The AMSTERDAM Cook Book

A celebration of the amazing food & drink on our doorstep.
Featuring over 35 stunning recipes.

The Amsterdam Cook Book

©2017 Meze Publishing. All rights reserved.

First edition printed in 2017 in the UK.

ISBN: 978-1-910863-39-8

Thank you to: Alain Caron, Café Caron

*Compiled by: Justin Brown, Julia Rameckers,
Nikki Burgers, Lorenzo De Corte, Julia Schols,
Charlotte Groenendijk, Coco van Bueren*

Written by: Kate Reeves-Brown, Kerre Chen

Photography by: Casper van Dort

Edited by: Phil Turner

*Designed by: Matt Crowder, Paul Cocker,
Jake Cowlishaw*

PR: Kerre Chen

*Cover art: David Broadbent
(www.davidbroadbent.co.uk)*

Contributors: Sarah Koriba, Laura Wolvers

Published by Meze Publishing Limited
Unit 1b Rialto
2 Kelham Square
Kelham Riverside
Sheffield S3 8SD
Web: www.mezepublishing.co.uk
Tel: 0114 275 7709
Email: info@mezepublishing.co.uk

Printed by Bell & Bain Ltd, Glasgow

FOREWORD

For me, we have to change food culture and serve affordable food to dissolve barriers and bring people together. The Netherlands is a country of innovation and in many ways ahead of its time; it has the appetite for a new kind of food culture, we just have to make it happen.

I have now been a chef for more than twenty-five years, and in that time I've been lucky enough to collaborate with many talented chefs from England, Japan, China, America, and Sweden. After growing up in the bustling metropolis that is Paris, being immersed in French culture and French cuisine, I craved new experiences, so I travelled a lot. I've worked in television, judged on Masterchef, written over thirty cook books, and worked as a magazine journalist.

My sons David and Tom came to me with the vision to open a café for all: a place for people to feel at home. Café Caron had to offer good food, good wine, pleasant surroundings and, above all, an affordable menu. It seems to be working, because we're full every day!

When all chefs speak the same language: a love of food, there can be no language barrier. I try to cook outside of The Netherlands as often as I can because I'm still learning the culinary language. I continue to be inspired by the people I meet and the places I visit and the flavours they unfold. I have a group of close friends I call Le Village de Chefs; chefs who actively cook and work outside of France. We keep in touch online to exchange our own unique concept of French cooking from each of our countries. This is the kind of community in which I like to immerse myself to keep in touch with the advances in French cuisine.

My French roots will always remain at the heart of my love for food – they form the basis of our cuisine at Café Caron, after all – but the world of food is constantly progressing, and I believe we have to grow with it. I fell in love with Amsterdam and its minor advancements, its dynamic culinary landscape and its quiet serenity. Amsterdam continues to feel like a new place to me; it's cosy – more like a cosmopolitan village with its small streets and shops, and that's what captured my imagination. I hope this appetizing book captures your imagination too!

Alain Caron

Co-owner of Café Caron

CONTENTS

Editorial

Credits 2

Foreword 4

The directory 146

The index 152

Chef recipes

ATL Seafood

Freshness assured 8

Roasted scallops with fermented garlic
mayonnaise and an oriental salad 11

Bao Buns Amsterdam

Take a bao 12

Pork belly bao buns 15

Blauw

The many flavours of Indonesia 16

Asam pade with corvina 19

Café Amoi

Selamat datang! 20

Ikan Pepesan 23

Café Loetje

Steak perfection 24

Biefstuk ossenhaas 'de Roode Waard' 27

Café Caron

A taste of La Café Caron 28

Escargots with monkfish fritters 31

The Chippy

Frying high 32

Fish and chips 35

De Drie Graefjes

Baking success 36

Pain Perdu 39

THE ENTOURAGE GROUP

Setting new standards 40

THE BUTCHER - So much more than
a burger bar 44

THE BUTCHER - Baby back ribs 47

THE DUCHESS - Caviar pasta 48

IZAKAYA - Red chilli and shiso salsa with
Dover sole 50

MOMO - Sashimi assortment 52

MR PORTER - Roasted whole leek 54

Grizzly

Food for the game 56

Mac 'n' cheese 59

The Harbour Club

True food meets glamour 60

Ceviche of sea bass 63

Herengracht

Home from home 64

Sea bass with groats, beetroot, sea aster, crunchy
smelt and sorrel foam 67

Het Warenhuis

Dining in style 68

Caramel and sea salt chocolate cake 71

Hotel Die Port Van Cleve

A history of hospitality 72

Famous numbered steak 75

Instock

Coming to the rescue 76

Chef Lucas' Wentelteefjes 79

Bubble and squeak 79

De Jonge Dikkert

Young and ambitious 80

Old Amsterdam cheese ravioli with
cauliflower and hazelnuts 83

JuiceBrothers

    Going green   84

    Acai almond bowl   87

Lavinia Good Food

    Simply good food   88

    Veggie meatballs   91

Le Pain Quotidien

    Breaking bread   92

    Chilli sin carne   95

    NY Cheesecake   95

Lt. Cornelis

    A taste of Dutch history   96

    Salted herring with beetroot and apple   99

Mamouche

    Mosey on down to Mamouche   100

    Moroccan chicken pastilla   103

Oresti's Taverna

    Mediterranean atmosphere   104

    Spanakopita   107

The Pancake Bakery

    Flippin' delicious - since 1973   108

    Bacon and apple pancakes   111

    Lemon and sugar pancakes   111

Pasta e basta

    Singing with your supper   112

    Green spaghetti with zucchini, asparagus, fresh seafood and panko gremolata   115

Pont 13

    Time to relax   116

    Cheesecake of white chocolate and yoghurt   119

REM Eiland

    One of a kind   120

    Soufflé of old Amsterdam   123

The Stillery

    Ancient craft   12

    The Mokum mule   127

Thai Food Cafe

    Have the Thai of your life   128

    Vegan pad thai   131

De Veranda

    A breath of fresh air   132

    Stuffed free-range chicken from the BBQ with za'atar and hasselback potato   135

Vida

    Living la Vida   136

    Pulpo horneado   139

Wild Moa Pies

    Wild about pies   140

    Awesome lentil and aubergine pie   143

Freshness ASSURED

ATL Seafood provide sustainable fish to some of the finest restaurants and chefs in Amsterdam.

The team at ATL Seafood all share a passion for the very best and freshest fish and seafood. Quality is key, but there is so much more to the success of the business than that – reliability, creativity, flexibility and durability are all hugely important to them, as well as their renowned friendly customer service.

ATL Seafood has a rich history within the culinary scene of Amsterdam. Amongst others, it is a partner of Momo Amsterdam, seafood restaurant Lucius Amsterdam, Bidvest Deli XL, Landal Greenparcs and Accor Hospitality Netherlands.

They know just how crucial quality ingredients are to chefs. All good chefs want to serve the best ingredients to their guests, and this passion is shared by ATL Seafood's own chefs, as well as everyone else in the team – drivers, representatives, production staff and office workers.

To ensure the high standards, fresh fish is purchased on a daily basis. Located next to the fish auction of Ijmuiden, they also source fish from various other auctions, as well as buying directly from the cutter ship GO 22.

Although the priority is for locally-caught fish, ATL Seafood also supplies fish from other parts of the world. This fish is treated with the utmost care and respect, believing that fish deserves the very best treatment throughout its journey from the sea to the kitchen. This includes careful production processes, for example, portioning fish fillets for customers who would rather buy an agreed weight in filleted fish.

Highly-trained and experienced staff who work in this production facility are always up to date with the latest developments. ATL Seafood is Food Safety System Certified 22000-2010 (FSSC 22000-2010), which means they have a quality system that guarantees the food safety of products from purchasing to distribution.

ATL Seafood is also a place where people can learn about fish. Their chefs are happy to provide on-site training, and people can also learn the art of filleting. Or for a less hands-on approach, they offer tours to demonstrate the journey the fish make from the sea to the kitchen. The tour takes in the fish auction of IJmuiden, a fishing boat and the company itself.

For customers interested in the sourcing of shellfish, they regularly organize visits to their suppliers in Zeeland.

Corporate social responsibility is at the core of ATL Seafood. Sustainable fishing is vital, and they work for a lasting solution to assure future fish stocks. ATL Seafood is MSC and ASCcertified and is working with the Dutch hospitality initiative 'Goede vis op de kaart' to assure customers receive sustainable wild and farmed fish. So, fish from ATL Seafood is not only a tasty choice, but also a sustainable one, too!

ATL Seafood
ROASTED SCALLOPS WITH FERMENTED GARLIC MAYONNAISE AND AN ORIENTAL SALAD

Go to your fish supplier and buy 12 fresh scallops and a bunch of razor clams to make this delicious dish of roasted scallops and an Oriental salad of razor clams, red pepper and lemon grass. You can ask your fish supplier to clean them for you.

Preparation time: 1 hour | Cooking time: 3 hours | Serves 4

Ingredients

For the scallops:

12 fresh scallops

Sea salt and pepper

For the Oriental salad:

A bunch of razor clams

1 bay leaf

Peppercorns

50g samphire

3 red chilli peppers

1 cucumber

3 purple potatoes

Coriander, to taste

Sushi vinegar, to taste

Salt

For the lemon grass foam:

50ml cream

50ml buttermilk

1cm piece of ginger

1 lemon grass

3 lemon leaves

For the fermented garlic mayonnaise:

2 egg yolks

1 tbsp mustard

2 cloves of fermented garlic

2 tbsp vinegar

500ml oil

Method

For the scallops

Clean the scallops or let your fish supplier clean them. Burn the scallops with a gas burner and season with a pinch of sea salt and pepper.

For the Oriental salad

Cook the razor clams for a few seconds in boiling water flavoured with the bay leaf and a few peppercorns. Clean the razor clams and cut the solid part of the razor clam into cubes.

Blanch the samphire for a few seconds in salt-free water, then clean them with cold water and chop them up.

Cut the red chilli peppers into thin strips and soak briefly in hot water. If you don't like spicy food soak the peppers a little bit longer. Cut the cucumber into fine strips.

Preheat the oven to 120˚c. Boil the potatoes until soft, then put them in the food processor with a little salt and olive oil and blitz until smooth. Spread the smooth potatoes out on baking paper and let them dry in the oven for about 3 hours. The dried potato will come away from the baking paper like chips, ready to decorate the plate. Set aside.

For the lemon grass foam

Boil the cream and buttermilk gently with the ginger, lemon grass and lemon leaves. Strain the cream after half an hour. Season to taste with salt. Use a cappuccino maker to turn the cooled cream into a foam.

For the fermented garlic mayonnaise

Mix the egg yolks, mustard, fermented garlic, vinegar and salt to taste. While beating, slowly add the oil to make mayonnaise.

To serve

Finally finish the salad by mixing the samphire, red chilli peppers, cucumber, razor clams, coriander and a little bit of sushi vinegar to taste. Serve with the scallops, potato chips, lemon grass foam and fermented garlic mayonnaise.

Take a BAO

Bao Buns, a pop-up street food concept from chef Justin Brown, is serving authentic bao buns, along with Taiwanese and Korean cuisine, all over Amsterdam.

Chef Justin Brown has always had a passion for the tastes, textures and aromas of Asian cooking. When he began doing pop-ups in Amsterdam, he would regularly feature fluffy homemade bao buns as one of the courses. At the time, there wasn't anywhere in Amsterdam serving authentic baos, and Justin received incredible feedback from diners, who always reported that the buns had been their favourite course of the evening.

This led Justin to do his first bao bun pop-up, which was an instant hit. Today, the trend has become so popular that bao buns are being served in various restaurants in the city, but what still sets Justin's buns apart from the rest is his dedication to making everything from scratch – from the buns and meat fillings to the kimchi, pickles and broths.

The buns are not straightforward to make from scratch, and customers can really tell the difference when they taste Justin's light and fluffy baos. The fillings change every week, although some of the firm favourites are always kept on the menu. The 16-hour pork belly, for example, is a classic, but other fillings can include chicken, tempeh, confit cod and crispy shrimp, and he sometimes adds a sweet fried bao to the menu for dessert.

The menu is tapas-style, so diners can select as much or as little food as they want, or there is the option to choose a 6-course menu. And it isn't all baos – there are plenty of other Asian dishes to try, including various ramen dishes, which have also taken the pop-up dining scene by storm.

Justin's Bao Buns pop-ups have become so popular that they can be fully booked up to two months in advance. As the location is always changing – taking in all corners of the city – Justin advises people to visit the website to find the next event and book a place in advance.

www.justinbrownchef.com/bao-buns.

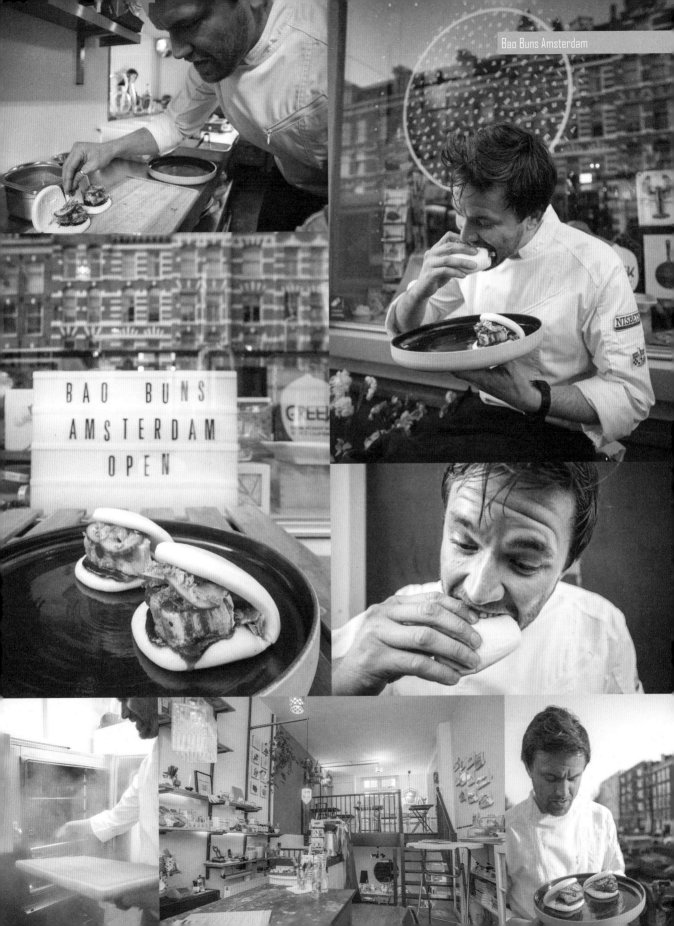

BAO BUNS
AMSTERDAM
OPEN

Bao Buns Amsterdam
PORK BELLY BAO BUNS

You can experiment with the fillings to go with the pork, if you like.

Preparation time: 1 hour 30 minutes
Cooking time: 3 hours and 15 minutes, plus 3 hours chilling | Makes: 20

Ingredients

For the filling:

1kg pork belly

2 bay leaves

10 whole peppercorns

10g mustard seeds

For the bao buns:

120ml milk

130ml warm water

6g dried yeast

20g caster sugar

490g plain flour

Oil

To garnish:

1 jar of hoisin sauce

1 cucumber, finely sliced

1 bottle of sriracha hot sauce

Method

For the filling

Preheat the oven to 170°c. Place the whole pork belly into a deep tray skin-side up. Cover the pork belly half way with water then add the bay leaves, peppercorns and mustard seeds to the tray. Place the tray into a preheated oven and cook for 3 hours.

Allow the pork to cool, then remove the pork belly from the liquid and remove any peppercorns, mustard seeds or bay leaves that may be stuck to the meat. Wrap the pork in cling film and place in the fridge for at least 3 hours to firm up. Keep the liquid for later.

For the bao buns

Heat the milk and water very gently in a pan to just above room temperature – it is very important that it is no hotter as it will kill the yeast. Remove from the heat, then add the yeast and sugar to the liquid and let it stand somewhere warm for 15 minutes. You will see the yeast activate and bubbles will appear on the surface.

After 15 minutes add the liquid to the flour and mix it to make a smooth dough. Place the dough somewhere warm for 40 minutes until it doubles in size.

Knead the dough for 10 minutes, then cut it into 45g pieces. Using the back of your hand, flatten each piece into a round shape, not too thin. Rub a little oil over the bao, then fold them in half. This create the right shape and also prevents them from sticking together. Place them on a lightly oiled tray, cover with oiled cling film and leave again to rise in a warm place for 25 minutes.

When ready to cook, steam the bao buns (in small batches) in a bamboo steamer on a piece of grease proof paper, covered with a lid, for 15 minutes. To reheat the buns later, just place them back in the steamer for 4–5 minutes.

To assemble

Heat the pork belly liquid in a pan. Slice the pork belly into pieces around 3cm thick, place in the pork liquid and simmer for a few minutes to warm up. Open the warm bao and spoon in some hoisin sauce. Place a slice of pork belly inside with a few slices of cucumber and cover with sriracha sauce.

The many flavours of INDONESIA

Blauw Amsterdam offers a taste of classic and contemporary Indonesian cooking in a modern restaurant setting.

Blauw Amsterdam opened nine years ago, following its successful sister restaurant in Utrecht. The two restaurants share the same friendly ethos, symbolised by the founder's family picture, which features on the wall of both venues.

Although there are many Indonesian restaurants in Amsterdam, Blauw has become famous for standing out in the crowd. On entering the restaurant, diners are met with modern décor. In fact, the contemporary interior doesn't give away its Indonesian menu at all. However, once the menus appear, customers are left in no doubt at all that they are about to enjoy some classic dishes from all over Indonesia.

Blauw serves dishes from Indonesia's many regions and islands, recognising that every island, town or village in Indonesia has its own unique specialities. Their saté kambing (goat satay) is everybody's favourite, even if some people are a little sceptical about it when they order. It is one of the dishes that the whole team loves, so they will advise guests to give it a go. The result? Most people will order some extra!

They also serve rijsttafels, which are popular for customers who are unfamiliar with Indonesian cuisine, but the à la carte menu is where the true taste of Indonesia resides. Dishes such as rendang are bursting with aromatic spices and are rich with authentic flavours.

The food at Blauw offers something for every taste and occasion. Although the kitchen is not halal (as they serve and prepare pork), all the meat that is delivered to them is halal. Indonesian cuisine is also a brilliant option for vegetarians and vegans, thanks to the vibrant mix of vegetables on the menu, as well as tofu and tempeh.

Indonesian authenticity doesn't end with the food. The drinks menu contains refreshing beverages like green iced tea and special tonics. Think only beers can be served with Indonesian cuisine? Think again. The wine list was chosen by the manager of Blauw Utrecht, a viticulturist who has expertly chosen the perfect wines to accompany the bold flavours of the food.

Many of the kitchen staff and waiters are from Indonesian backgrounds, and the whole Blauw family shares a passion for Indonesian cuisine. The young and dynamic team are known for being full of energy, and their approach to friendly service has earned them a reputation for always going the extra mile.

Blauw
ASAM PADE WITH CORVINA

Asam pade is one of the most famous dishes in Padang (West Sumatra). It has gained its popularity in Indonesia because of its many components. The spices and herbs in this dish balance out for a great taste! And for a meal this tasty, it's surprisingly easy to make.

Preparation time: 20 minutes | Cooking time: 20 minutes | Serves 4

Ingredients

1kg corvina fish

100ml oil

8 shallots, thinly sliced

4 garlic cloves, sliced

3 asam kandis (or 100g tamarind paste)

150ml water

2 lemon grass (sereh) stalk, bruised

1 turmeric (kunyit) leaf

For the paste (boemboe):

8 red chillies (lomboks)

6cm fresh ginger (djahe)

4cm fresh turmeric (kurkuma)

4cm fresh galangal (laos)

Method

Cut the fish into firm pieces, about 6 cm. Grind the paste (boemboe) ingredients together until you have a paste.

Slowly heat the oil in the wok. Once the oil has reached the right temperature, add the shallots and garlic slices. Next, add the paste and let it cook for 3 minutes on a low heat. Add the water, followed by the lemon grass, turmeric leaf and the asam kandis. Let it cook for 7 minutes.

Now it's time to add the fish. Let it boil for approximately 10 minutes on a low heat and season to taste. The dish is now ready to be served – it is delicious served with white rice.

Selamat
DATANG!

A warm welcome awaits at Amsterdam's newest Indonesian eatery, Café Amoi.

Café Amoi opened its doors in September 2016 on the Kinkerstraat in Amsterdam West. A contemporary Indonesian restaurant, it serves authentic Indonesian food alongside Indonesian-inspired drinks. The name, Amoi, means 'younger sister' – which is exactly what Café Amoi is. It is the younger, more modern sister of the well-known restaurant Sarang Mas, which is now closed.

Café Amoi began life with the aim of not doing things the old-fashioned way. Where Sarang Mas was traditional, Café Amoi is playful and modern. The founders, Felix and Willemijn, opened the restaurant with the help of their friend Danny. Felix was the owner of Sarang Mas, so he had lots of knowledge when it came to devising the menu for Café Amoi, as well as the help of some of the chefs from his previous restaurant.

Working together, Felix and Willemijn took a fresh approach to modern Indonesian dining. They thought creatively about the design of the restaurant, as well as the type of food they would serve. The result was an innovative shared dining menu which includes delights such as duck spring rolls, rice rolls with spiced mackerel, lamb skewers, and sea bass grilled in banana leaves.

The chefs in the kitchen are known as 'tantes'. They are elderly Indonesian ladies who simply love to cook; not only at the restaurant, but also at home during the day. They know everything about authentic Indonesian flavours – you can smell that as soon as you walk into Café Amoi. Close your eyes for a second and you could almost be in Indonesia. These talented ladies work with some younger chefs, too, which creates a perfect balance of traditional and modern elements; authenticity and creativity.

Flavoursome spicy dishes need a refreshing drink alongside, and at Amoi the drinks list is quite an impressive selection. Try an Indonesian-inspired cocktail with homemade spekkuk liqueur, ginger beer and white sipping rum, perhaps? They also serve authentic Bintang beers, as well as non-alcoholic drinks like fresh coconut water of Teh Botol iced tea.

The bartenders enjoy playing with Indonesian spices, such as cloves, cardamom, ginger and kaffir lime leaf, so the drinks are just as aromatic and flavourful as the dishes coming from the kitchen. Café Amoi is a feast for all the senses.

Café Amoi

Café Amoi
IKAN PEPESAN

A delicious whole sea bass is baked with spicy bumbu paste in a banana leaf.

Preparation time: 10 minutes | Cooking time: 20 - 25 minutes | Serves 2

Ingredients

For the bumbu paste:

1 white onion, peeled

2 garlic cloves, peeled

10 candlenuts (kemiri noten)

5 red chilli peppers

1 tbsp ginger, chopped

½ tsp ground white pepper

½ tsp tumeric powder (koenjit)

1½ tbsp vegetable oil

Pinch of salt

Large pinch of sugar

For the sea bass:

1 banana leaf

1 whole sea bass

1 lemon grass, chopped (sereh)

2 kaffir lime leaves

To serve:

White rice

Cucumber in vinegar

Method

For the bumbu paste

Put all the ingredients for the bumbu paste in an electric food mixer and mix for 5 minutes until you have a paste.

For the sea bass

Preheat the oven to 180˚c. Take the banana leaf and cut a piece that is big enough to wrap the sea bass. Make sure the banana leaf is dry and clean. If not, use a clean towel to dry it. Take 2-3 tablespoons of the bumbu paste and spread it in the middle of the banana leaf. Put the sea bass on top of the paste. Again put 2-3 tablespoons of bumbu paste over the sea bass. Make sure you spread enough paste on the fish. Take the lemon grass and kaffir lime leaves and put them on the sea bass and on the paste for some extra flavour.

Now roll the banana leaf around the sea bass as a package. If you want to make sure that the paste won't drip out of the banana leaf, use some aluminium foil over the banana leaf. Make sure it is wrapped well. Now bake it in the oven for 20-25 minutes.

To serve

This is nice served with white rice and cucumber in vinegar on the side.

Steak PERFECTION

Known throughout Amsterdam for its famous steak, Café Loetje has become a culinary landmark thanks to its 40-year history of delicious food and friendly hospitality.

Although it is today one of Amsterdam's best-loved eateries, Café Loetje actually started life 40 years ago as a neighbourhood pub and billiards bar on the corner of the Johannes Vermeerstraat in Amsterdam South, near the Museumplein.

Customers could enjoy a fry-up, a meatball or a serving of cheese at Café Loetje, but it soon became apparent that regulars had an increasing desire for a more substantial plate of food. The tenderloin steak was introduced – and the rest is history.

The owner's background in butchery certainly came in handy, as the steak was a big success. The billiard tables were replaced with dining tables and the 'new' café filled up every day with fans of the 'Loetje steak'.

Café Loetje has evolved over the years, growing and developing a more modern look, while keeping a number of characteristic elements from its past. The façade is authentic; diners can eat at special 'Loetje tables' and the old logo is still visible on the windows – a nod to the billiards bar of the past.

Today Café Loetje is a cosy restaurant with a spacious seating area, bar, pleasant dining room and an outdoor terrace where people can sit amidst the hustle and bustle of Amsterdam.

As the reputation of the tastiest steak has spread far and wide, Café Loetje has become a favourite with both locals and tourists who are keen to sample the delicious dish. This has allowed them to expand into other locations around the city and across The Netherlands.

One of these is Loetje Centraal, which is located in a beautiful historic building on the Stationsplein, right in the heart of Amsterdam. Its location opposite the Central Station and near the Tourist Information Centre and Canal Company makes it a great place to meet up and enjoy a delicious bite to eat before going out into the city – or somewhere to round off a day of sightseeing with a good meal.

Bright, spacious and homely inside, the restaurant's interior boasts typical Dutch and Delft blue elements, including the tap at the bar. Situated right on the water, the view is a real bonus. Take in the lively Prins Hendrikkade from the cosy outdoor terrace – there is always something to see as tour boats and private barges pass the restaurant. This is a place to soak up the feeling of being at the heart of Amsterdam.

Café Loetje
BIEFSTUK OSSENHAAS 'DE ROODE WAARD'

A taste of the famous Loetje steak to try at home... perfectly cooked tenderloin steaks are served with crispy bacon, flavoursome chicken livers and fried onion rings.

Preparation time: 5 minutes | Cooking time: 20 minutes | Serves 4

Ingredients

200g chicken livers, halved

300g fried onion rings

300g bacon slices

200g good-quality margarine, preferably Blue Band

4 tenderloin steaks, 200g each

Salt and white pepper, to season

Oil, for frying

1 onion

Method

Firstly, prepare the chicken livers by frying them over a high heat. Make sure that they are still a little pink and keep them warm.

Fry the bacon until crispy and warm the onion rings.

Heat up the margarine in the frying pan over the highest heat. In the meantime, season the steaks with salt and pepper. Put them in the pan as soon as the margarine has stopped sizzling and sear them for about 1 minute on each side.

Lower the heat and keep moving the steaks around with tongs in the gravy for 2–3 minutes more, depending on the desired rareness of the meat. Take care that the gravy does not burn.

Take out the steaks when ready and place them on a platter with the chicken livers around. Make a nice emulsion of the gravy by stirring it well in the frying pan, then pour it over the steaks.

Finally serve with the warm fried onions and the bacon on top.

A taste of La
CAFÉ CARON

Café Caron brings a little touch of France to the quirky streets of Amsterdam, promising high quality, affordable food and beverages and a cosy, relaxed ambience.

Café Caron is the pride and joy of talented chef Alain Caron and his sons, Tom and David. Situated in the heart of Amsterdam, the café is a kind of home-from-home, serving up simple yet satisfying French cuisine, with vegetarian options readily available, too.

In 1983, Alain ventured to the Netherlands and developed a strong respect and appreciation for Amsterdam's culture. Now, he considers himself a self-proclaimed 'Dutch-French', with a wealth of experience from his time as a chef in Paris and his collaboration with chefs from all over the world. Alain passionately advocates that there can be no language barrier in the kitchen when chefs all speak the same language: a love of food. It's this appreciation for good food and a desire to champion affordable dining which fuelled the inspiration for opening Café Caron.

The versatile and seasonal menu offers a variety of dishes – fresh oysters (one of Alain's personal favourites), fried duck egg and fall truffles served with palm cabbage, Trompette de la Mort mushrooms with a sprinkling of Parmesan and chicken thighs drizzled in eel sauce, served with chicory and mashed potatoes, just to name a few. Each dish carries a visual aesthetic which pays homage to Alain's brief time studying art, proving that good food can look just as good as it tastes. And the wine flows generously too, with 46 different bottles to complement each dish on the menu, from Champagne to Sauvignon Blanc, Pinot Noir and Italian red wines, to a sweet Bordeaux.

Promising nothing less than a high-quality sumptuous meal for each and every person that walks through its doors, the establishment is a constant full house and this is after being open for only a few months.

Family is the most important ingredient here, the Caron family have gone to great lengths to make their establishment an open and relaxing space, eager to nurture the art of dining out and promote the beauty of French cuisine. This is a fitting example of two generations coming together to create something special, and it certainly appears to be working!

Café Caron

Café Caron
ESCARGOTS WITH MONKFISH FRITTERS

This fairly simple recipe looks best when presented on a deep plate to allow all the different elements of the dish to truly come together in a striking array of colours and textures.

Preparation time: 20 minutes | Cooking time: 90 minutes | Serves 4

Ingredients

For the snails:

2 tbsp olive oil

24 cooked snails

4 garlic cloves, finely chopped

A lump of butter

3 tbsp beef gravy

¼ bunch parsley, finely chopped

Salt and pepper, to season

For the monkfish fritters:

16 small chunks of monkfish

125g flour

30g cornflour

15g baking powder

5g salt

175ml beer

For the watercress coulis:

½ bunch organic watercress

1 bunch parsley

1 tbsp Dijon mustard

1 soft boiled egg

150ml chicken stock

A pinch Xanthan gum (binder)

A pinch of salt

For the garlic cream:

2 garlic bulbs, cleaned

Dash of whipped cream

Salt and pepper, to season

To garnish:

8 La Ratte potatoes, peeled and sliced

A knob of clarified butter

Lemon, slices

A few twigs of watercress

Method

For the snails

Heat the olive oil in a frying pan and warm up the snails on a high heat.

Next, add the ingredients in the following order: garlic, butter, gravy, parsley, at 30 second intervals, keeping on a high heat. Turn the heat off just before all the moisture is absorbed by the snails, and season with salt and pepper.

For the monkfish fritters

Chop the pieces of monkfish (preferably the cheeks) about 1cm x 1cm, cook them in salted water and then let them cool. Mix the flour, cornflour, baking powder, salt and beer in a bowl with a whisk until it becomes a smooth batter. Immerse the pieces of monkfish in the batter, and fry in oil at 190°c until golden brown.

For the watercress coulis

Add all the ingredients to a blender and combine until it comes together as an even green mixture, then add a pinch of salt.

For the garlic cream

Put the cleaned cloves of garlic in a pan of cold water over a hob, once it is boiling, pour the water out and repeat this process two more times. Once your garlic is boiled, add a dash of whipped cream and mix thoroughly before seasoning with salt and pepper.

To serve

In a saucepan, stir the small potatoes in some clarified butter and gently cook them at a low temperature.

Grab a deep plate and smear with a thin layer of the warm garlic cream, then drizzle the watercress coulis around it. Alternate six snails, four monkfish fritters and two potatoes in the centre of the plate.

Finish off with a slice of lemon and a few sprigs of watercress for garnish.

Frying HIGH

Traditional British fish and chips has been popping up all over Amsterdam, courtesy of Justin Brown and The Chippy.

When British chef Justin Brown moved to Amsterdam, one of the things he missed the most was the classic English dish of fish and chips. Fresh cod, haddock or plaice encased in a crisp beer-batter is synonymous with the British seaside – it conjures up memories of tucking into piping hot chips and steaming fish straight out of newspaper on the seafront.

May 2016 saw The Chippy's first pop-up in West Amsterdam. Justin chose the name 'The Chippy' to convey the style of the food he would be serving up. The many British people who live in Amsterdam immediately associated 'The Chippy' with a taste of home, and the first pop-up was an immediate success. Local newspapers featured The Chippy during its initial run and, thanks to incredible reviews, the pop-up became one of the city's most coveted places to dine.

The concept might be British, but the fish is sourced from the Dutch coastline to ensure only the freshest fish makes it onto the menu. Freshly-caught cod, haddock and plaice take centre stage, accompanied by a range of homemade sides. Chips – of course – are essential for most customers, but there

are plenty of other options too. Justin and his team pickle their own eggs and onions, and make their own mushy peas, tartare sauce, gravy and curry sauce.

As well as traditional battered fish, there is also the lighter option of grilled fish, as well as some non-fish dishes, including homemade pie, battered chicken goujons and the famous battered sausage.

If diners still have room for dessert, The Chippy's ice cream sundae is perfect for sharing between two people – or to challenge one hungry person! They have also taken a leaf out of Scotland's book and serve battered Mars Bars and Snickers… gooey chocolate bars encased in crisp batter – this is something that everyone should try at least once in their lives!

Keep an eye on the website to see where The Chippy is popping up next, as it continues to take a taste of the British seaside all over Amsterdam.

www.thechippy.nl

The Chippy
FISH AND CHIPS

Beer-battered haddock, homemade chips, tartare sauce and mushy peas. Go to your local fishmonger to buy your fresh fish, they will remove all the little pin bones from the fillets for you and be able to help you with choosing your fish. I like to use haddock, but any white fish works well.

Preparation time: 40 minutes | Cooking time: 20 minutes | Serves 4

Ingredients

For the tartare sauce:

3 free-range egg yolks

1 tsp white wine vinegar

½ lemon, juiced

350ml virgin olive oil

2 large gherkins, roughly diced

½ bunch parsley

3 tbsp capers, drained

Black pepper

For the chips:

6 large Maris Piper potatoes

Vegetable oil, for frying

For the beer batter:

350g plain flour

6g dried yeast

150ml light beer

150ml sparkling water

Pinch of sea salt

For the mushy peas:

300g frozen peas

200ml double cream

To serve:

1 lemon, cut into wedges

For the fish:

4 fillets fresh haddock, skin on, 150g each

Seasoned flour, for dusting

Method

For the tartare sauce

To start the tartare sauce, take a tall jug and place the egg yolks, white wine vinegar and lemon juice in it. Take a stick blender and blitz for 1 minute. After 1 minute, very slowly add the olive oil, blitzing constantly, and the egg will slowly emulsify with the oil forming a mayonnaise (You may not require all the oil.) Once the mayonnaise thickens, add the gherkins, capers and parsley, and season with black pepper. Blitz for a minute until everything is mixed. If it is too thick, add 2 tablespoons of cold water and blitz for 30 seconds to thin it down slightly, then tip into a container and chill until needed.

For the chips

The chips can be made in advance and re-cooked when needed. Peel and cut the potatoes into 1cm sticks (peeling is optional, you can give the potatoes a good scrub and leave the skins on). Place them in a bowl and run them under cold water for 5 minutes to remove the starch. Place the chips into a pan of water and bring to a simmer. Cook for 1 minute, strain into a colander and leave to cool for 10 minutes. Once cool, tip them out onto a kitchen cloth to remove any excess water.

Heat a deep fryer to 130°c. Fry the chips in vegetable oil for 5 minutes, until a chip pierces easily with a knife. Remove and leave to cool on a rack. At this stage, you can place them into the fridge for up to 24 hours.

For the beer batter

Sift the flour into a bowl, add the dried yeast then whisk in the beer and sparkling water until you have a nice thick, smooth batter. Season with a pinch of sea salt and set aside.

For the mushy peas

Boil the peas for 1 minute, then strain and place the peas into a food processor and blitz with the cream for 1 minute. If you like your mushy peas chunkier, heat the peas in a pan with the cream and mash with a potato masher.

For the fish and to serve

Heat a deep fryer to 180°c. Coat the fish in seasoned flour and tap any excess off, then place into the batter. Lift out of the batter and gently and carefully lower into the oil. Fry the fish for about 5-6 minutes until golden and crisp, then remove with a slotted spoon and drain on kitchen paper. Once all the fish is cooked, add the chips. Fry for 3-4 minutes until golden and crisp, drain on kitchen paper and sprinkle with sea salt. Place a piece of fish on each plate, add some chips and serve with a wedge of lemon, some tartare sauce and a side of mushy peas.

Baking SUCCESS

De Drie Graefjes, a lunchroom and American bakery, has been serving breakfast, lunches and cakes, as well as high tea, in the heart of Amsterdam for 16 years.

When it comes to fresh ingredients, friendly service, mouth-watering breakfasts, hearty lunches and a central location, there is nowhere that ticks the boxes quite like De Drie Graefjes. The story began in 2001 when Ferdi opened a lunch room just behind Dam Square, serving internationally inspired dishes and shortly after, high teas as well.

By 2008, the business had become extremely successful, so when the premises next door became available, Ferdi jumped at the chance to take over the site and opened a bakery in the adjoining space. The bakery specialised in American cakes and desserts, and it was an instant hit.

Ferdi was joined by his daughter Aylin in 2009, who came on-board full-time at De Drie Graefjes when she finished her education, having always helped out at weekends and after school. In 2011, the father-daughter team opened a second lunch room at Rokin, followed by a bakery with a full production kitchen next door in 2014.

Today Aylin leads the operational side of the business which retains a strong family-focus – her father still works in the development side of the business, her mother helps with interior décor and design, and her sister-in-law is also a key member of staff.

They have built up a strong reputation amongst locals, who love the satisfying breakfasts (from homemade granola to American pancakes) and hearty lunches (we're talking club sandwiches, juicy burgers, fresh salads, homemade soups and melting toasties). With their central location, they are also a popular spot for tourists, who are impressed by the generous portions of freshly-cooked food which is served at non-touristy prices. In fact, many travellers will come back time and time again during their stay in Amsterdam!

From savoury to sweet, there is no end to the options at De Drie Graefjes. The takeaway bakeries at both Rokin and Dam Square can satisfy any sweet tooth. New York cheesecake, brownies, gluten-free cupcakes, carrot cake, blueberry muffins, red velvet cake, blondies… all of these and more are made fresh each day.

And for something a little more luxurious, the kitchen at Rokin also welcomes you to sit down and enjoy a luxurious high tea. Served beautifully on tiered cake stands, guests can enjoy fine teas while indulging in a selection of mini sandwiches, quiches and soup, followed by mini scones with cream and homemade jam, finished off with some delicious pastries. For an extra-special treat – why not add a glass of prosecco, too?

De Drie Graefjes
PAIN PERDU

Although the Dutch have a reputation for being thrifty, 'Amsterdammers' are not very keen on eating stale bread. Luckily there is a sugar-coated way to turn your spiritless leftovers in to a heavenly breakfast dish. For centuries people have been recycling their 'lost' bread by soaking it in milk. Then the Romans came up with the unconventional idea to fry the soaked bread and sweeten it with honey. This improvement went down so well that stale bread became sparse and no longer 'lost'.

The first recognition of French toast in The Netherlands was in a sentence in old Dutch that dates back to 1623: 'Ey, waer ick t'huys alles, ick backte wentelteven van suyckert witte brood, en butter-smeerigh vet.'

At De Drie Graefjes we replaced the stale bread with authentic Frisian sugar bread. By using this gooey kind of bread, we give an extra sweet and soft touch to the French toast we serve in our lunchrooms. Once you've had this pain perdu with fresh fruit you will never want another kind of breakfast again!

Preparation time: 10 minutes | Cooking time: 10 minutes | Serves 6

Ingredients

18 slices of Frisian sugar bread, about 1.5cm thick

1 litre whole milk

5 eggs

1 tbsp ground cinnamon

1 tsp vanilla sugar

Pinch of salt

Butter, for frying

Seasonal, fresh fruits (e.g. strawberries, kiwi, banana), to serve

Icing sugar, to serve

Method

Cut the 18 slices of sugar bread (3 slices per serving). Whisk together the milk, eggs, cinnamon, vanilla sugar and salt in a medium-sized bowl and set aside.

'Dunk' each slice of bread in the egg mixture and let it soak for 2 minutes. Melt one tablespoon of butter in a large non-stick frying pan over medium to medium-high heat.

Gently remove the sugar bread from the egg mixture and place them in the frying pan straight away. Fry each side until golden brown and crispy.

Continue frying the rest of the slices, adding extra butter when needed. Top the French toast with fresh fruit and/or icing sugar.

Setting new STANDARDS

Since 2008 the hospitality industry in Amsterdam has been led by THE ENTOURAGE GROUP, who are now taking their Amsterdam-born brands across Europe and changing the face of modern fine dining.

Yossi Eliyahoo is the man behind THE ENTOURAGE GROUP, a hospitality brand that has become renowned in Amsterdam for its internationally acclaimed high-end restaurants and bars. The story began in 2008 when Yossi opened MOMO, a pan-Asian restaurant which went on to win awards for its highly celebrated cuisine, bar and cocktail lounge.

MOMO not only established pan-Asian cuisine in Amsterdam, but it also brought the concept of shared fine dining to the city. Yossi has a unique view on hospitality and a creative vision, so he didn't shy away from trying new ideas – and he has been rewarded with many successes.

MOMO was followed by IZAKAYA, a contemporary Asian dining experience that set new standards for Japanese cuisine with its inventive dishes and beautiful surroundings. IZAKAYA's concept is of sharing dishes, and it also embodies one of THE ENTOURAGE GROUP's signature concepts

– bringing the classic and the contemporary together. Using time-honoured techniques and blending them seamlessly with innovative and contemporary ideas, IZAKAYA has become known for its cutting-edge twists on authentic Asian cuisine. The restaurant introduced Nikkei cuisine to the city, where extravagant Japanese cuisine meets Latin American flavours.

From here Yossi set his sights on street food – how could he bring a little of THE ENTOURAGE GROUP magic to something as simple as a burger? THE BUTCHER was born in 2012 and it has quickly shaken up the casual dining scene with its approach to high-quality fast food. So incredibly successful was the first restaurant that THE BUTCHER soon expanded to include four locations in Amsterdam and mobile food truck THE BUTCHER On Wheels. The Amsterdam-born concept has even expanded outside of the city, with new locations in Berlin and Ibiza.

The latest additions to the group are THE DUCHESS and MR PORTER. THE DUCHESS was a leap away from trendy burger joints and high-end Asian cuisine, to an awe-inspiring refined elegance – proof of Yossi's diverse experience in the industry and appreciation of all types of food. Set within the breath-taking former KAS Bank building, THE DUCHESS is a lavish dining experience that befits its stunning location, complete with a huge dining hall, stained glass ceiling and marble columns. From elegant afternoon teas to classic lunches inspired by Southern France and Italy, THE DUCHESS became synonymous with style and elegance soon after opening. Like the other venues within THE ENTOURAGE GROUP, the drinks list plays a crucial role here. From Champagne and award-winning cocktails to a well-selected wine list, the bar has won various awards for its offering.

MR PORTER opened in 2015, bringing another twist to Amsterdam's culinary collection. This sophisticated steak house has raised the bar for fine dining in the city. Located at the top of the former exchange building, MR PORTER embraces duality in everything it does, exploring the contrast between simplicity and extravagance in its food and drinks. With award-winning cocktails and a DJ playing at weekends, MR PORTER brings something fresh and exhilarating to Amsterdam's eating and drinking choices.

Yossi has become known as one of Amsterdam's most innovative entrepreneurs, winning 'Hospitality Entrepreneur of 2015' in The Netherlands' prestigious Entrée Hospitality Awards. With years of experience in the industry behind him, having worked in restaurants in Tel Aviv, New York and London, Yossi knows that the key to his success is this knowledge of the business. Not only in cooking amazing food and drinks, but finance, management and brand development.

"As a creative concept developer, I envision and feel the places I design before they actually exist. I love to develop something from the roots and pay attention to every tiny detail. Every aspect has to be captured by the same language," said Yossi Eliyahoo.

He is now taking his Amsterdam-born brands across Europe, and with it, flying the flag for the Amsterdam food and drink industry. He says: "The hospitality industry of Amsterdam is growing and developing at an incredible speed. It has been, and still is, a pleasure to be part of that change. When I entered the Dutch scene, I was determined to establish a revolutionary level of quality and service. Now we aim to do it the other way around. Brands like THE BUTCHER, IZAKAYA, THE DUCHESS and MR PORTER will now enter and join international markets."

So much more than a
BURGER BAR

From its trade-mark urban style to its unique branding and excellent food THE BUTCHER offers a unique high-end fast food experience in various locations around Amsterdam.

Nowhere has shaken up the fast food scene in Amsterdam quite like THE BUTCHER. Since the first location on Albert Cuypstraat opened in 2012, THE BUTCHER has quickly built a reputation for serving the best burgers in the city, along with a generous helping of charisma and style.

High-end yet casual, trendy yet relaxed, finest quality yet cooked up in a flash, THE BUTCHER manages to combine all these elements with ease, describing itself as, "so much more than a burger bar". It's no wonder it has become one of the city's favourite eateries.

The concept was created by renowned hospitality entrepreneur Yossi Eliyahoo, who put craftsmanship and top-quality ingredients at the heart of the business from day one. The 'butchers' in the kitchen are lucky enough to work with the best Aberdeen Angus beef when crafting the burgers. When this carefully selected meat is combined with the freshest herbs and vegetables, the special signature sauce and homemade semi-brioche bun, the end result is something worthy of recognition – in fact, it was awarded 'best burger of Amsterdam' by Time Out magazine.

The success of the first restaurant led to the opening of THE BUTCHER West, located in the Foodhallen, in 2014, followed by food truck THE BUTCHER on Wheels, THE BUTCHER Nine Streets and THE BUTCHER Social Club in 2016. The Social Club is open 24/7 on weekends, with live music, a vintage video games hall and a huge terrace overlooking the IJ river. This Amsterdam-born eatery is now taking the brand across Europe with a branch in Berlin and an exciting new opening in Ibiza in summer 2017.

Each individual location of THE ENTOURAGE GROUP has its own unique personality and charm, but the design-led style, distinctive branding and excellent service runs through each venue. The trade-mark life-size cow hangs in the window and the traditional butchery elements are used with great effect in the simple, modern and stylish interiors. The open kitchen design allows customers to watch the 'butchers' craft the food in front of their eyes.

As the team behind THE BUTCHER reminds us, there is so much more to them than the burgers. Along with the laid-back vibes, great music, cool interiors and relaxed atmosphere, they have become known for their impressive shakes, smoothies and cocktails, too. THE BUTCHER Social Club in Amsterdam North features an island bar serving beers, cocktails, spirits and more. In fact, THE BUTCHER is rumoured to be serving some of the city's best cocktails – just what is needed to accompany their award-winning burgers.

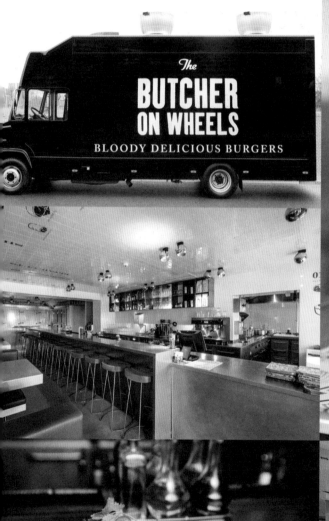

The Butcher
BABY BACK RIBS

We use Iberico baby back ribs because they have a lot of meat on them.
However, if they are not available, any baby back pork ribs can be used instead.
The meat needs to be marinated in the rub 2 days before cooking.

Preparation time: 20 minutes, plus 2 days marinating | Cooking time: 4 hours and 20 minutes | Serves 2

Ingredients

For the ribs:

2 racks Iberico back ribs

60g salt

40g sugar

20g smoked paprika

½ tsp garlic powder

½ tsp onion powder

For braising the ribs:

1 carrot, roughly chopped

¼ celery root, roughly chopped

1 white onion, roughly chopped

1 leek, roughly chopped

1 star anise

1 clove

Small cinnamon stick

¼ jar sambal ketchup

For the BBQ sauce:

250g sambal ketchup

150g honey

1 lime, juice

Method

For the ribs

Mix all the dry ingredients together to create the rub, then rub the mixture onto the ribs, making sure that all sides are coated. Place them in a tray, wrap with cling film and leave in the fridge for 2 days.

For braising the ribs

Preheat the oven to 100°c. Place the rubbed ribs in a deep baking tray. Add the roughly chopped vegetables to the tray, along with the spices, and cover it with water. Cover the tray with a lid or aluminium foil. Place the tray in the oven for 4 hours.

Remove the baking tray from the oven and let the ribs cool down in the cooking liquid. When the temperature has come to room temperature, carefully remove the ribs from the liquid and place in a dry tray. Place in the fridge to cool.

For the BBQ sauce

Mix all the BBQ sauce ingredients together.

To finish and serve

Preheat the oven to 200°c. Place the ribs on a baking tray lined with parchment paper. Brush the ribs with the BBQ sauce on both sides. Roast in the oven for 20 minutes, brushing with BBQ sauce every 5 minutes. Transfer the ribs to a plate and serve. Enjoy!

The Duchess
CAVIAR PASTA

From breakfast classics through to light lunches, elegant afternoon teas and decadent dinners, THE DUCHESS is a luxurious dining experience set within the grand splendour of one of Amsterdam's architectural gems. Sitting beneath high ceilings within the historic former KAS Bank building, surrounded by the opulence of gold and marble, this is the perfect setting to indulge in fine cuisine inspired by Southern Italy and Southern France.

The light, refined flavours of these Mediterranean cuisines are showcased in the delicate cooking at THE DUCHESS. Guests can watch the chefs at work in the open kitchen, while they enjoy an aperitif or glass of fine Champagne. The afternoon teas have earned a reputation for their charm and decadence, with beautiful teapots and tiered cake stands adorning the tables. Combining the elegance of the past with the innovation of the contemporary, THE DUCHESS is a place where past and present come together for sumptuous results.

This dish is quick to make and is very impressive to serve to guests with the luxurious addition of Oscietra Caviar.

Preparation time: 10 minutes | Cooking time: 20 minutes | Serves 1

Ingredients

50ml white wine

1 shallot, peeled and chopped

1 sprig fresh thyme

6 black peppercorns

50ml whipping cream

50g cold butter, cut into small cubes

1 tsp fresh lemon juice

2g salt

70g dry spaghetti

2 tsp chives, chopped

7g Oscietra Caviar

Method

In a small saucepan over medium heat, add the wine, shallot, thyme and peppercorns. Reduce almost completely until a thick syrup is formed.

Add the whipping cream and reduce by half. Pass this reduction through a fine sieve and into another, bigger, saucepan set over medium heat.

Whisk in the butter, one cube at a time, until fully incorporated with the cream. Do not boil. Remove from the heat and season with the lemon juice and salt.

Meanwhile, boil the spaghetti for 8-9 minutes, to the desired doneness (al dente). Drain the spaghetti in a sieve and then, while hot, toss the spaghetti in the sauce until well coated. Add the chives and combine.

Twirl the pasta with a pair of thin tongs into a tight roll. Slide onto a dinner plate and pour extra sauce around the plate decoratively. Finish the pasta with the caviar on top, and serve immediately.

Izakaya
RED CHILLI AND SHISO SALSA WITH DOVER SOLE

IZAKAYA Kitchen and Bar is celebrating five years of reinventing time-honoured Japanese cuisine in De Pijp. This innovative restaurant concept is part of hospitality entrepreneur Yossi Eliyahoo's renowned hospitality empire THE ENTOURAGE GROUP. Along with managing director Stephanie Pearson, Yossi has created a unique and innovative dining experience where authentic Japanese techniques are combined with Latin American and contemporary twists.

From its signature Robata grill to its menu of grazing-style small plates, IZAKAYA takes inspiration from the distinctive elements of Asian and Latin American culinary culture. Cutting edge design features, an extensive cocktail list and chic international ambience have given IZAKAYA a reputation for being a spectacular place to enjoy food and drink. Its stunning design has seen it win 'Most Beautiful Bar' at the Entrée Hospitality awards in 2014 – a harmony of lines, colours and shapes around the 360° bar create the perfect setting to enjoy fine Japanese cuisine.

The simplicity of pan-fried Dover sole is the perfect choice to accompany the zingy and spicy red chilli and shisho salsa.

Preparation time: 20 minutes | Cooking time: 10 minutes | Serves 1

Ingredients

For the red chilli and shiso salsa:

20g red onion, finely chopped

10g red chilli, finely chopped

4 shiso leaves, finely sliced

40g red shiso vinegar

15g green tabasco

10g grapeseed oil

½ lime, juice

For the Dover sole:

1 piece Dover sole, 300-350g, skin on

Flour, for dusting

Olive oil, for frying

Salt and pepper

Method

For the red chilli and shiso salsa

Mix all the chilli and shisho salsa ingredients carefully and stir well.

For the Dover sole

Remove the skin from the Dover sole and carefully cut all four fillets. Season the Dover sole fillets with pepper and salt. Put flour on both sides of the fillets and shake off the excess flour.

Heat a non-stick pan over medium heat. Use a little olive oil to sauté the fillets on both sides until golden brown.

To serve

Scoop the red chilli and shiso salsa on a plate. Carefully place the filets on top of the salsa and serve immediately.

Momo
SASHIMI ASSORTMENT

For the creator of MOMO, Yossi Eliyahoo, there is so much more to creating a fabulous restaurant than the food alone. The founder of hospitality specialists, THE ENTOURAGE GROUP, had the full dining experience in mind when he opened MOMO in 2008. The award-winning pan-Asian restaurant, bar and lounge, defined a new standard in Dutch hospitality from day one.

The creative menu features nigiri, sushi, sashimi, ceviche and tiradito, along with signature dishes like black cod with spicy miso or scallops and edamame with XO sauce. Award-winning bartenders tell a story with each inventive drink, and they have an impressive selection of sake served alongside.

A unique combination of beautiful interior design, cutting-edge culinary skills and an international ambience, MOMO continues to strive for perfection in every aspect of the business.

You need the very freshest fish for sashimi. If the inside of the fish eyes are clear like fresh water then it's fresh. Alternatively, open the gill of the fish and look inside. If the inside is a bright red colour it is fresh; if it is brownish red then it is not suitable for this dish.

Preparation time: 20 minutes | Cooking time: 10 minutes | Serves 1

Ingredients

For the tako:

1 piece octopus leg

For the shime-saba:

1 fresh mackerel fillet

100g fine salt

500ml Japanese rice vineger (shira-giku)

To serve:

30g fresh salmon fillet

30g fresh hamachi (yellow tail) fillet

40g fresh yellow fin tuna fillet

1 fresh sea bass fillet

2 lemon slices

1 lime slice

1 shiso leaf piece

1 oyster leaf piece

200g daikon (Japanese radish)

10g Osicetra Caviar

Method

For the tako

Add the octopus to a pot of boiling water, but as soon as you add the octopus, you need to keep the temperature at around 90°c – do not let it boil. Cook for 30–40 minutes, then take the pot off the heat and leave the octopus in the water until it reaches room temperature. Then place in the fridge.

For the shime-saba (vinegared mackerel)

Take out the small bones fromt the middle of the mackerel fillet. Cover the fillet with fine salt and leave it at room temperature for 1-1½ hours. Wash the salt off the mackerel and then soak it in rice vinegar for 20–30 minutes. Dry out the mackerel with kitchen paper.

To serve

Slice all the fish with a very sharp sashimi knife into three slices. You need to slice the octopus thinner than the other fish. Plate all the fish and garnish as you like on the plate with the lemon and lime slices, shiso leaf, oyster leaf, daikon and caviar. For the best effect, serve it on crushed ice or a cube of ice (you can make a cube of ice in a milk carton).

Mr Porter
ROASTED WHOLE LEEK

The fine dining steak house MR PORTER is a medley of contradictions – it is simple yet extravagant, traditional yet always surprising. Part of THE ENTOURAGE GROUP, it was founded by hospitality entrepreneur Yossi Eliyahoo: "It is at the intersection of the familiar and the unknown, where real magic happens. MR PORTER captures that truth and translates it into a culinary experience unlike any other."

The unique concept combines the irresistible qualities of a modern steakhouse with the atmosphere of a cocktail lounge, which has seen it win various awards for its unrivalled design and offering. Located on the rooftop of the former exchange building, it enjoys a unique vantage point befitting of its chic design. It has become known as the perfect setting to enjoy succulent steaks, homemade side dishes, an array of innovative fish and vegetable dishes and sumptuous, sinful desserts. Resident DJs create the ideal background atmosphere for the stylish surroundings. MR PORTER represents modern fine dining at its best.

This is a beautifully simple way of tasting the delicious flavour of leek. Some garlic, lemon juice, olive oil and a sprinkling of Maldon sea salt is all that is needed.

Preparation time: 20 minutes | Cooking time: 10 minutes | Serves 1

Ingredients

1 thick leek

1 garlic clove

1 lemon, juice

5 tbsp olive oil

Maldon sea salt

Method

Preheat the oven to 220°c.

Cut off and discard the green part of the leek. Carefully cut off the roots without harming the flesh of the leek. Wash the leek under cold running cold water to remove any dirt.

Place the leek on a metal baking tray and roast it in the preheated oven for 10 minutes. Turn it over and roast it on the other side for a further 10 minutes.

Remove the leek from the oven and place it on a chopping board. With a very sharp knife make an incision along the leek's skin, but do not harm the flesh. Be careful, as it will be very hot and hot steam might be released when you open the skin.

Remove the leek flesh from the skin onto your chopping board. Slice the leek into six bite-size pieces.

Place the skin on a plate. Put the sliced leek back on to the skin, so that the skin is part of the plating.

To serve

Crush the garlic in a garlic crusher. Mix with the lemon juice and olive oil. Drizzle the dressing over the leek using a spoon. Sprinkle a little Maldon sea salt over it. Enjoy!

Food for THE GAME

In the heart of Amsterdam's famous Red Light District, Grizzly is an all-American restaurant and bar where you can enjoy major sporting events while tucking into some of the best state-side food.

Grizzly opened in one of Amsterdam's most vibrant districts, Warmoesstraat 64, in August 2016 in the former home of one of the city's most famous coffeeshops, Coffeeshop BABA. When the city of Amsterdam's policy meant that all of the coffeeshops in Warmoesstraat had to be closed, the idea was born to create a new restaurant and bar in this busy street.

Stepping in from the hectic road outside, guests are welcomed into a lively space that features multiple large screens for sports. Whether it's the Superbowl or the NBA finals, all major sporting events are shown on the big screens at Grizzly.

If it's not sport you are interested in, take a seat at one of the tables and set your sights on the food instead. From breakfast through to lunch and dinner, the menu is jam-packed with mouth-watering dishes. Enormous breakfast portions will set you up for a day seeing the sights – from pancakes to bacon and eggs.

Lunch and dinner can consist of a variety of classic American dishes. Try salmon, steak or grilled chicken, or opt for their famous mac 'n' cheese, the recipe that they have shared in this book. The burgers are always popular, served with freshly cooked fries and a crispy salad.

A wide range of speciality beers, liquors and wines complete the meal, unless you have got room for a mouth-watering dessert of course… and Grizzly is known for serving those American palate-pleasers that are simply impossible to resist.

One thing that continually sets Grizzly apart in a city that is full of great places to eat is its amazing team of friendly staff. No matter how busy this small restaurant gets, the bartenders love to chat to customers and never fail to have a smile on their faces.

With hearty American food, a great selection of drinks and a welcoming atmosphere, Grizzly provides something totally different in one of Amsterdam's busiest districts.

Grizzly MAC 'N' CHEESE

This is such a delicious and rich dish that is simple to make at home. Make sure you use the right cheeses and the right maccheroni for the dish. It is great served with chicken wings on the side!

Preparation time: 10 minutes | Cooking time: 40 minutes | Serves 4

Ingredients

For the mac 'n' cheese:

2l milk

2l cream

500g grated cheddar

500g blue cheese, crumbled

500g Parmesan cheese, grated, plus extra to serve

50g onion powder

50g garlic powder

1 tbsp mustard

Salt and pepper

1.2kg maccheroni

200g lettuce

Handful of cherry tomatoes

For the chicken wings Grizzly-style:

200g ketchup

200g chilli sauce

1 tsp paprika powder

100g ketjap

Salt and pepper

1kg chicken wings

Method

For the mac 'n' cheese

Heat the milk and the cream in a pan. Once cooked, add the cheeses and stir until you have a smooth sauce. Add the spices and the mustard and season with salt and pepper. Stir until you get a nice, thick consistency.

Bring a pan of water to the boil, then add a little salt. Immediately add the maccheroni to the pan. Boil for 3 minutes or until cooked, then drain the maccheroni in a colander.

Add the maccheroni to the sauce and give it a good stir so that it is well mixed. Divide the mac 'n' cheese between four plates and finish the dish with some lettuce, a few cherry tomatoes and some grated Parmesan.

For the chicken wings Grizzly-style

Mix the marinade ingredients together, add the chicken wings and let them marinate for a few hours in the fridge. Preheat the oven to 180°c. Cook the chicken wings in the preheated oven for 30 minutes or until the chicken is cooked through. Serve while hot.

True food meets GLAMOUR

Premium, tempting and stylish... meet The Harbour Club Amsterdam East!

The Harbour Club began life in 2008 with the opening of The Harbour Club Scheveningen, a restaurant situated in the always-busy yacht harbour on the Dutch coast. Its interior is a surprising combination of old and new that is reminiscent of the old fish market. In the following nine years, four more unique locations of The Harbour Club opened their doors: The Harbour Club Rotterdam (2010), The Harbour Club Amsterdam East (2012), The Harbour Club Amsterdam South (2015) and, their youngest sister, The Harbour Club Vinkeveen (2017).

The Harbour Club Amsterdam East was the third location to be opened, in 2012, unique of its kind because of its location in an old wine terminal. Again, a fascinating location that forms a blend between Miami, Barcelona and the Côte d'Azur. This is an old wine terminal turned fashionable chic, where, in the old days, they were bottling the wine, they now uncork them!

The restaurant has an extraordinary ambiance with international allure, a vibrant atmosphere and extraordinarily great food. You'll be amazed by the immense space, the top-notch styled interior, the high-quality cooking, the six-metre-long fish display case and the famous murals from neo-pop art artist Selwyn Senatori.

The signature dishes of The Harbour Club Amsterdam East form the basis of the menu. Thanks to its setting in the harbour, having fresh fish daily is the most natural of things at The Harbour Club, mainly using fish caught that very day. Only the finest ingredients are good enough, which is why they visit specialised suppliers on a regular basis to stay completely up to date on the products they offer to their guests.

They combine high-quality cooking with a dash of playfulness, but always with an eye for detail. The preparations are simple and pure: meat from the open Josper grill, sole baked in real butter, and grilled lobster. For sushi and sashimi, the best farmed Blue-Fin tuna is purchased from Malta. But for super fresh oysters and platters of fruits de mer, The Harbour Club is the place to be. Meat lovers can enjoy the exclusive dry-aged Tomahawk steak.

Did you know they even have their own The Harbour Club Gin? A taste explosion infused with wasabi, cucumber and sea salt. Such a pleasure to mix with tonic water!

The Harbour Club guarantees 100% satisfaction with the help of over four hundred inspired and passionate employees. Service with a genuine smile – The Harbour Club prides themselves on quality and hospitality.

The Harbour Club
CEVICHE OF SEA BASS

This delicate dish is light and fresh, and it will impress dinner guests. Make sure to use the very freshest sea bass you can find.

Preparation time: 40 minutes | Serves 2

Ingredients

For the sea bass:

200g wild sea bass

For the dressing:

60ml yuzu juice

100ml soy sauce

5cm kombu

250ml water

1 orange, juiced

40g sugar

For the avocado cream:

½ avocado, stone removed

½ lime, juiced

20ml olive oil

Salt and pepper, to taste

For the garnish:

2 or 3 cherry tomatoes

40g mango

A few coriander leaves

¼ red onion

½ red pepper

Method

For the sea bass

Cut the sea bass fillet in thin slices and set aside until you are ready to prepare the plates.

For the dressing

Mix all the ingredients for the dressing and let steep for 30 minutes. Remove the kombu after 30 minutes.

For the avocado cream

Place the avocado together with the lime juice, olive oil, salt and pepper in a blender and purée. Put the mixture in a piping bag and store in a cool place.

For the garnish

Cut the cherry tomatoes into quarters and then finely dice the mango. Pick the leaves off of the coriander. Remove the seeds of the red pepper and cut into thin rings. Cut the red onion julienne style. Take a mixing bowl and mix all the ingredients, then add the dressing to the mixture.

To serve

Serve the sea bass in slices on a plate, accompanied by the garnish mixture and finish with the avocado cream.

Home from HOME

A canal-side restaurant and bar with beautiful terraces, Herengracht has been welcoming locals and tourists to the canal district for 14 years.

Sipping a glass of wine or local Dutch beer by the canal is a quintessential picture of Amsterdam life – and nowhere makes this experience quite as charming as Herengracht. Named after the canal by which it resides, this central bar and restaurant is a welcoming spot that allows people to escape from the hustle and bustle of the city and enjoy some classic hospitality.

Herengracht Restaurant & Bar was opened by Niels and Colette Reijers in 2003, and has been run by Wessel Kuipers and Alex Permeke since 2013. A long-time favourite spot for people who work nearby, Herengracht is known as a place which is ever-welcoming, whether it is for a drink in the bar, some light snacks, a meal in the restaurant or a cocktail in the garden.

It has built a reputation for its atmosphere and service. Despite its prime location in one of Europe's most famous cities, it is known for being unpretentious, warm and inviting. For a large space, they have created a unique cosiness in the split-level layout – from the downstairs bar to the main restaurant, the décor is rich with wood, leather and warm colours, along with interesting copies of old paintings made with recycled materials on the walls. Locals compare it to being in a cosy yet chic living room, where they are welcomed like one of the family.

As well as the canal-side terrace, Herengracht also boasts a light garden room that leads out to an inner courtyard, exemplifying the many faces of Herengracht Restaurant & Bar. There are no rules here – you are welcome to come for drinks, for lunch, for snacks, for dinner – the personable team will make sure that guests enjoy the experience, whatever time of day and whatever they order.

The approach to food at Herengracht is centred on good, honest cooking. French-style dishes are made with locally sourced Dutch ingredients, and everything is made from scratch each day.

What makes this restaurant stand out in a city that is full of talented chefs and fine food? For Wessel and Alex, it is about giving customers the whole experience. The food will be great, the drinks will be interesting, but most importantly, the vibe will be truly memorable. And this is what they hope guests will remember long after the last mouthful of delicious food.

Herengracht
SEA BASS WITH GROATS, BEETROOT, SEA ASTER, CRUNCHY SMELT AND SORREL FOAM

This dish is a typical example of the kind of dishes we like to prepare at Herengracht. A modern, hearty French-style recipe with lots of local products. The use of ingredients such as the salty sea aster, beetroots and sorrel shows the diversity of what Holland has to offer, and gives this dish a homely feel.

Preparation time: 15 minutes | Cooking time: 30 minutes | Serves 4

Ingredients

For the groats:

Olive oil, for frying

1 garlic clove, finely chopped

½ carrot, finely chopped

½ leek, finely chopped

2 celery stalks, finely chopped

250g groats

100ml white wine

½l vegetable stock

2 tsp crème fraîche

For the sorrel foam:

½ litre fish stock

1 bag of sorrel

A splash of cream

100g butter, cold and cut into cubes

Salt and pepper

For the smelts:

1 bag of tempura flour

100ml sparkling water

32 smelts

For the sweet and sour beetroot:

2 Chioggia beetroot

100ml white wine vinegar

100ml water

100g sugar

For the sea bass:

4 sea bass fillets, with skin

To serve:

120g sea aster

Method

For the groats

Heat two tablespoons olive oil in a thick-bottomed pan and sear the garlic, carrot, leek and celery lightly. Add the groats and stir well, then deglaze with the white wine.

Let this simmer for a few minutes, then add enough of the vegetable stock until the groats are just covered with liquid, and stir well. Continue to cook, adding more vegetable stock until the grain is soft and cooked.

For the sorrel foam

Meanwhile heat the fish stock in a separate pan, add the cut sorrel and let this stew for some time. Remove it from the heat, then add a dash of cream and some lumps of cold butter. Then, using a blender, blend the sauce lightly to create a light foam. Add pepper and salt to taste.

For the smelt

Mix the 50ml sparkling water with the tempura flour and make sure there are no lumps. Season to taste with salt. This is your batter. Heat the oil for deep-frying in a heavy-based pan or deep-fryer. Pull the smelt through the batter and fry them in the hot oil carefully, in batches. Drain on kitchen paper.

For the sweet and sour beetroot

Slice the beets in very thin slices using a mandoline or cheese slicer. Cook the water, sugar and vinegar together and let it cool. Put the beetroot in this mix and leave it for 30 minutes until it becomes sweet and sour.

For the sea bass

Sprinkle salt on the sea bass. Heat a frying pan with a little olive oil and sear the fillets in the hot pan, skin-side down and cook until the skin is crispy and the meat is no longer shiny and transparent but still juicy.

To finish and serve

Mix the crème fraîche with the groats and place over a very low heat. Sear the sea aster briefly in a hot pan with a little oil.

Divide the groats evenly amongst four deep plates and top each portion with a sea bass fillet, skin-side up. Add the smelt and sea aster. Garnish with the Chioggia beetroots and the foamy sorrel sauce. Enjoy your meal.

Dining IN STYLE

In the midst of one of Amsterdam's most elegant and chic neighbourhoods, Het Warenhuis is the perfect place to enjoy a meal in style.

The shop window of Haarlemmerstraat 65 does not showcase flirty skirts, sharply cut suits or polished shoes. Het Warenhuis presents a collection of classic brunch dishes and international bites to share. Cups o' Joe and cocktail classics are more fitting accessories. Seated behind the immense window lounging on the stretched sofa or working at one of the shared tables, Amsterdam meets, drinks and dates at Het Warenhuis.

In times long gone, the façade of the corner building on the Haarlemmerstraat read 'Manufacturen-Magazijn WILLEM III'. This historical site was a department store selling fabrics, blankets and coats. Years later, the lobby of the Quentin Arrivé Hotel, situated on the upper floors of the building, moved into the store, until the owners of the hotel decided to give the place back to their neighbourhood. They designed Het Warenhuis: a place fitting the local community, and most of all, the Haarlemmerstraat. A place where a freelancer puts away his or her laptop at the end of the day to swap coffee and sandwiches with wine and bites. A place of comprehensive hospitality.

Het Warenhuis lifts casual eating to a new level, from brunch until drinks. The culinary catalogue consists of scrumptious brunch food as well as international classics and platters to share. The collection ranges from eggs benedict or florentine to Black Angus burgers or the all-time favourite mushroom risotto. Daily, Het Warenhuis dresses up brunch time with a spicy bloody Mary or refreshing mimosa.

Furthermore, Het Warenhuis breaks the boundary between online and offline hospitality. As one of the first restaurants Het Warenhuis launched a lifestyle web-shop, following the 'what you see offline, you can buy online' concept. Everything you see in the restaurant – from lamp to floor tile – you can order online using the QR-codes.

The window that once was supposed to increase the sales of vibrant fabrics now displays the scenery of (re)connecting visitors and residents of the Haarlemmerstraat. It's a setting in which the eclectic crowd exploring the neighbourhood meets, greets and dines.

Het Warenhuis
CARAMEL AND SEA SALT CHOCOLATE CAKE

Luxurious and rich, this decadent chocolate cake has a salted caramel topping.

Preparation time: 20 minutes | Cooking time: 30 minutes | Serves 10-12

Ingredients

For the cake:

100g Tony's Chocolonely dark chocolate

100g Tony's Chocolonely caramel & sea salt

180g unsalted butter

100g sugar

6 eggs

3 tbsp flour

For the caramel sea salt topping:

100g sugar

50ml water

40g unsalted butter

50ml cream

1 tsp Maldon sea salt

Method

For the cake

Preheat the oven to 180°c. Grease and line a cake pan.

Melt the 200g chocolate together with the butter in a heatproof bowl set over a pan of boiling water. Remove the bowl from the heat and add the sugar. Add the eggs, one by one, and give it a good mix. Stir in the flour. Pour the batter into the cake pan and bake in the oven for 20 minutes.

For the salted caramel topping

Put the sugar and the water in a saucepan. Let it simmer on low heat until it has a brownish caramel colour. It's hard, but try not to stir! Add the butter and mix it all through. Add the cream – there will be a bubble explosion, but don't worry, that's supposed to happen. Remove from the heat. At this point the caramel will be quite runny. If you let it cool down, you will get a thicker caramel paste. Both consistencies are delicious on the cake.

To finish

When the cake is cooled, pour the caramel over the cake. Sprinkle as much Maldon sea salt on top as you like.

A history of HOSPITALITY

From its home in the original Heineken brewery, Hotel Die Port Van Cleve tells a story that dates back over 100 years – a story of passion, dedication and 6 million steaks...

More than a century ago there were two very capable men, who came across a special location in Amsterdam which they immediately fell in love with. We're talking about the birthplace of the beer brand Heineken. Back in 1864, Gerard Heineken bought 'De Hooiberg Brewery', which he sold a few years later in order to grow. The people he sold it to? Our founders, the Hulscher brothers.

Continuing the legacy of their predecessor was not their only intention. They wanted to exceed it and eventually conquer the whole world. There was however, one problem... they didn't know how. But this wasn't the only issue, the brothers turned out to have very dissimilar characters and ideas for their new property. While their mum tried to bring them together by telling them that they were just "the best of two worlds", they grew further apart than ever before and a success story seemed just an illusion.

In time, they agreed on the idea to start a restaurant called Die Port Van Cleve, but continued to disagree about what to serve. Meat or fish? Beer or wine? Their discussions peaked at the end of 1869... During a night out after many beers, they blamed each other for all kinds of things. What started with

a simple comment about each other's appearance would have ended in a fight if it wasn't for Wilma's intervention. Neither of them could remember Wilma the morning after, but it was her who brought them back together. That night back in 1869 turned out to be the start of a genuine Amsterdam success story.

From day one in September 1870 the brothers served the most sophisticated steaks and seafood in the whole country. Even in the remotest corners of the Netherlands people were aware of the existence of the delicacies served by the brothers. Due to the overwhelming success, they couldn't keep up the pace and that's why they served all their steaks with a unique numbered certificate.

The story is still going strong within this mind-blowing building. The brothers left the world with something extraordinary and the numbered steak is still on the menu. Even the certificates remain the same. The only things that have changed are the numbers on them.

Meat or seafood? Like their mother once said: "Why not have the best of both worlds!"

HULSCHER'S

AMSTERDAM 1870

FAMOUS STEAK – PREMIUM GRILL – SEAFOOD BAR

Hotel Die Port Van Cleve
FAMOUS NUMBERED STEAK

"Our famous numbered steak didn't become famous just because of the little certificates. Nope, it's way more than just a number. It's all about passion, love and of course my genuine and sophisticated sense of taste." G.J. Hulscher.

Preparation time: 10 minutes | Cooking time: 10 minutes | Serves 1

Ingredients

For the steak:

1 diamond fillet

Butter, for cooking

Salt and pepper, to taste

For the béarnaise sauce:

100g egg yolks

50ml gastrique (caramelised sugar deglazed vinegar)

200ml melted butter

Tarragon, finely chopped, to taste

Lemon juice, to taste

Tabasco sauce, to taste

Worcestershire sauce, to taste

Salt and pepper, to taste

Method

For the steak

To start with you'll need to develop the most sophisticated sense of taste possible. I know that might be difficult, but please try if you want to impress your guests. The diamond fillet is the most tender meat you can get on the market, especially if you follow these instructions... The diamond is the cut of meat situated between the shoulders of a cow. In The Netherlands, we call it 'Jodenhaas'.

Enter the kitchen like a true chef and own that part of your home for the rest of the day. Preheat the oven to high. Bring the steak to room temperature, season it with a little bit of salt on both sides, but be as gentle as can be.

Make sure you preheat your pan and use good-quality butter to make the most out of this pure work of art. After a brief pause, the butter will get a nice brown colour, which means it's your moment to shine. Carefully place the steak in the middle of the pan. Are you done? No! Most certainly not! Be careful not to underestimate this part of the process... Scorch the steak for a maximum of 1½ minutes on both sides and turn it with tongs. Transfer the pan with the scorched steaks to the hot oven and roast the steak for 3-5 minutes (depending on how you like your steak cooked). Tent your masterpiece loosely with aluminium foil and give it a well-deserved rest for 5 minutes. After all of this, the only thing you can do is pray your steak has reached the quality of the steaks that we serve in our restaurant. If desired, you can use a little pepper and salt as a finishing touch.

For the béarnaise sauce

You're almost done... you've already given it your all, I know. However, this will make it even better! Beat the egg yolks and the gastrique with a whisk over a bain-marie. Cook it over a low heat, whisking constantly until the mixture thickens and forms thick ribbons. Remove the pan from the heat and slowly pour in the butter in a thin stream. Stir in the finely chopped tarragon. Season to taste with salt, pepper, lemon juice, droplets of Tabasco and Worcestershire sauce. There you go, victory has arrived. Use your sauce immediately or keep it warm (don't push it). Now it's your time to impress someone with the result.

Enjoy and please pass by one day, my brother and I will welcome you with open arms.

Coming to THE RESCUE

With one-third of all food produced being wasted through the food chain, the team behind Instock decided to come to the rescue of all that surplus...

Instock is the name behind a team of food superheroes who are saving surplus food, one ingredient at a time. The idea began in 2014 when the founders were working for a large food retailer. They were all united by the passion for sustainability and reducing food waste, and the amount of surplus food that was wasted in their store drove them to research what could be done about it.

Food that was perfectly edible was passed over by customers who would always select the perfectly formed vegetables, while leaving any misshapen ones on the shelves. When they began to research this problem, they found that supermarket waste accounted for only 5% of food waste. 39% of food waste happens at the producer side, before it even gets to the shops, restaurants or our homes. 42% of food waste occurs in households and about 14% in the hospitality branch. Time for change across the whole food chain!

Instock began with a pop-up restaurant in 2014 with the simple mission of rescuing surplus food. By 2015 they opened their first restaurant in Amsterdam and today they are proud to have another two restaurants to their name in The Hague and Utrecht, as well as a food truck for event catering.

The secret to success comes down to the creativity and passion of the chefs. Using flavours from cuisines around the world, they take inspiration from each day's harvest to create delicious dishes. The team love to promote this way of cooking – looking at what ingredients you have to hand and then deciding what to cook. In this way, they have turned the standard idea of cooking (choosing a dish and then going to buy the ingredients) on its head, replacing it with freedom and creativity.

They believe food should tell a story, and this is something they encourage in their own cookbook. They have become known for preserving food, and their cookbook shares many tips on pickling and drying, for example. Not only do these ancient techniques make food last longer, but they also give it an extra oomph when it comes to taste.

The latest development at Instock was the launch of their locally brewed beer, Pieper Beer. Made with potatoes that would otherwise have been wasted, this ingenious craft beer is raising the bar when it comes to giving rescued food another lease of life. And from the leftovers of beer (spent grain) they make their own granola! Try 'beer for breakfast' in their restaurant.

INSTOCK

BREAKFAST & LUNCH
CEREAL AND FRUIT, FRENCH TOAST,
SALAD AND MORE

DINNER
THREE OR FOUR COURSES
MADE WITH THE HARVEST OF THE DAY

COFFEE & DRINKS
TRY OUT OUR PIES OR BITES TO SHARE

Instock

Take me home

INSTOCK
CAFÉ RESTAURANT

Photo: Arnout Gijzeñ?

Instock

CHEF LUCAS' WENTELTEEFJES

Yesterday's croissant dipped in crème brûlée makes a delicious meal. We serve it with burnt banana, banana compote and a butterscotch sauce.

Preparation time: 15 minutes | Cooking time: 15 minutes | Serves 6 - 8

Ingredients

500ml cream

75g sugar

½ tsp cinnamon

Pinch of salt

75g egg yolk

75g whole egg

6-8 leftover croissants

Butter, for frying

Icing sugar, for dusting

Burnt banana, to serve

Method

Warm the cream in a pan. Meanwhile whisk the rest of the wet ingredients in a bowl. Pour the hot cream over the other ingredients while whisking. Strain and set aside in the fridge. Soak the croissant in the cream mixture for 3 minutes, then place in a hot pan with a little butter and cook until golden brown; around 2 minutes on each side.

To serve

Spread a little cream on a plate, set the croissant beside it and scatter burnt banana slices around the place. To finish off, dust with icing sugar.

BUBBLE AND SQUEAK

A fantastic way to turn those leftover veggies into a tasty meal. Serve it with your favourite sauce!

Preparation time: 10 minutes | Cooking time: 10 minutes | Serves 4 - 5

Ingredients

2 tbsp olive oil

400g leftover veg (about half potatoes, then Brussels sprouts, carrots, turnips)

Smoked bacon, fish or tempeh, cooked and chopped

1 egg, to bind

Sea salt and freshly ground black pepper

Method

Heat the olive oil in a pan. Mash together all the remaining ingredients then shape it into 4-5 portions. Cook the bubble and squeak in the hot oil until golden. Alternatively, you can crumb it and deep-fry it instead. Serve with your favourite delicious sauce.

Young and AMBITIOUS

Having held a Michelin Bib Gourmand since it opened 24 years ago, De Jonge Dikkert boasts superb internationally inspired cuisine within a 17th-century windmill.

When De Jonge Dikkert first opened, its aim was to provide really good food at a good price. The ambitious team was rewarded in the first year with a coveted Michelin Bib Gourmand – an accolade it holds to this day, making it the longest held in The Netherlands.

The restaurant is set within an iconic windmill. Although the mill dates back to 1672, once people step into the restaurant they tend to be surprised by the elegant contemporary interior. The cosy ambience welcomes everyone who wants to enjoy a good plate of food – seven days a week the restaurant is packed with locals, tourists, families, couples, groups of friends and work colleagues. Whether people are enjoying a quiet supper, a family celebration or a business meeting, the relaxed setting allows everyone to be themselves.

The team takes pride in the contemporary design of the restaurant. Being up to date and at the forefront of modern European dining is important to everyone at De Jonge Dikkert. They are members of JRE (Jeunes Restaurateurs), which is an association of passionate and talented young European restaurateurs and chefs.

The contemporary décor is reflected in the food, as well as providing the perfect backdrop for the dishes to shine. The international menu takes inspiration from around the globe, while using ingredients sourced locally. Around 80% of the produce used in the kitchen at De Jonge Dikkert is grown or made in The Netherlands. Amsterdam is lucky to have access to incredible fish from the North Sea, as well as oysters and scallops, which can be served fresh from the ocean.

A commitment to using local produce means that the menu also follows the seasons, making use of the freshest seasonal ingredients available, and as much as possible is organic. As far as the food in concerned, the philosophy is to keep the ingredients recognisable on the plate. There is no need to make the dishes too fancy when the cooking speaks for itself.

Set just 15 minutes from the bustling centre of Amsterdam, yet only 15 minutes from the airport, De Jonge Dikkert is an easily accessible destination for award-winning dining.

De Jonge Dikkert

OLD AMSTERDAM CHEESE RAVIOLI WITH CAULIFLOWER AND HAZELNUTS

This delicious ravioli of Old Amsterdam and cauliflower is served in a mushroom broth and accompanied by roasted cauliflower, sweet and sour cauliflower, Jerusalem artichoke chips, chives, hazelnuts and grated purple cauliflower.

Preparation time: 60 minutes | Cooking time: 60 minutes | Serves 3

Ingredients

For the pasta:
150g flour

50g pasta flour

10g olive oil

150g egg yolk

For the filling:
75g cream

1 gelatine sheet

25g crème fraiche

235g Old Amsterdam, finely sliced

10g pasta flour

100g cauliflower, grated

½ bunch parsley, chopped

½ bunch chervil, chopped

Salt and pepper

For the broth:
200ml brown chicken stock

50g dried mushroom

For the Jerusalem artichoke crisps:
500ml soybean oil

1 Jerusalem artichoke, thinly sliced

For the cauliflower:
50g sugar

100ml white wine vinegar

1 white cauliflower

100g butter

To serve:
50g hazelnuts

½ bunch chives, chopped

1 purple cauliflower

Method

For the pasta
Mix the flour, pasta flour, olive oil and egg yolk. Instantly add 75ml water and season with salt and pepper. Wrap in cling film and place in the fridge.

For the filling
Heat the cream and dissolve the gelatine in the hot cream. Put the crème fraîche, Old Amsterdam and the 10g pasta flour together into a food processor. Add the cream and blitz on high speed until you have a smooth cream. Strain the cream, then add the grated cauliflower and herbs. Season with salt and pepper.

For the broth
Bring the chicken stock to the boil, add the dried mushrooms and cook until the stock has reduced by half to about 100ml.

For the Jerusalem artichoke crisps
Heat the soybean oil to 180°c. Fry the thin slices of Jerusalem artichoke until golden brown and crispy.

For the cauliflower
Put the sugar and white wine vinegar in a pan with 1½ cups of water, and bring to the boil. Take half of the white cauliflower, cut it into florets, add to the sour liquid and cook for 1 minute.

Melt the butter in a pan until it is golden brown. Take the other half of the white cauliflower, and cut it into florets. Add to the butter and fry until cooked.

To serve
Toast the hazelnuts in the oven for 10 minutes until coloured, then chop coarsely.

Divide the pasta dough in half and roll it into two long, thin sheets. Coat with egg yolk. Place the filling on one length of the pasta dough, then cover with the other sheet of pasta dough and cut out.

Cook the ravioli for 6 minutes in boiling water, then add to the mushroom broth. Serve with the Jerusalem artichoke crisps, roasted cauliflower, sweet and sour cauliflower, roasted hazelnuts and chives. Finally, shave the purple cauliflower using a microplane and add to the dish.

Going GREEN

Cold-pressed juices, smoothies, bowls and nutritious snacks, JuiceBrothers is bringing a taste of New York to Amsterdam with its 100% organic products.

Since it opened two years ago, JuiceBrothers has been replenishing thirsty Amsterdammers with their certified organic juices and bowls, as well as a variety of other tasty treats. The concept was the idea of Noah Boeken, Bibi Janus and Guus Benning, who fell in love with cold-pressed juices during their travels in LA, New York and various other cities around the world.

Instead of complaining about the lack of cold-pressed juice bars in The Netherlands, they decided to do something about it. Two years of research, experiments and endless taste tests followed before they eventually opened JuiceBrothers in the Spring of 2015.

The flagship store is a vibrant haven of health and vitality. As well as being the first place in the city to sell cold-pressed juice, they are also proud to be certified organic, which was hugely important to them when they set about creating their business. As well as organic, their produce is also totally vegan… and utterly tasty!

The welcoming environment of the store is a feast for all the senses. Friendly staff are happy to allow customers to sample juices before buying them. They can also advise people on detox cleanses, which can give the digestive system a break and leave you feeling revitalised and refreshed.

It is all about helping people reach the optimum level of health. As well as using only organic produce, they make everything fresh from scratch, including their own 'mylks', granola, raw bliss balls and other healthy sweet treats. Their bowls are extremely popular for breakfast – an acai bowl packed with fruit and granola makes a superbly nutritious start to anybody's day.

When it comes to their cold-pressed juices, the vibrant range creates quite a rainbow of colours. From the ruby red shade of Dragon's Breath (made with pear, apple, carrot, grapefruit, beetroot, lemon and ginger) to the bright green of Force of Nature (consisting of cucumber, celery, spinach, kale, parsley and lemon), the juices are easily absorbed into the system as they require no digestion.

Since they opened their first store two years ago, JuiceBrothers now have six branches across Amsterdam. In 2017, they welcomed a franchise in New York, and Noah, Bibi and Guus plan to take their Amsterdam-born brand to many more locations in the future.

JUICEBROTHERS

At JuiceBrothers, we use the cold-pressed method for juicing. Fruits and vegetables are shredded and hydraulically pressed, with minimal generation of heat and thus minimum oxidation. Heat kills many of the vitamins, minerals and live enzymes you think you're getting when consuming other "healthy" juices. The cold-press method allows enzymes to stay alive, resulting in juice with maximum nutrients.

Making you feel good is our main goal. We'll never judge you or tell you how to live your life. Whether you're grabbing a hydrating juice to replenish you after yoga or to revive you after a long night out, it's all good! Go ahead, take a sip.

#juicebrothers

JuiceBrothers
ACAI ALMOND BOWL

Use organic ingredients to make this 100% organic acai almond bowl, which is simple to whip up at home.

Preparation time: 5 minutes | Serves 1

Ingredients

For the acai almond bowl:

120g banana, frozen

100g acai, frozen

70g almond milk

20g almond butter

10g honey

For the toppings:

JuiceBrothers granola

Cacao nibs

Goji berries

Sliced banana

Almond butter

Method

Blend the frozen banana, frozen acai, almond milk, almond butter and honey together, then place into a bowl.

Top with your choice of toppings – JuiceBrother granola, cacao nibs, goji berries, sliced banana and almond butter.

Simply
GOOD FOOD

Lavinia Good Food opened her doors at the Kerkstraat 176 in 2014 with the desire to serve organic, fairtrade and healthy good food.

In 2001, the founders of Lavinia Good Food, Karel Hessing and Sonia Philipse, started a high-end catering company called Food Fantasies, which mainly focuses on serving corporate clients at the highest level. Food Fantasies is, however, more than a catering company; it's a culinary design studio producing food for a clientele that has seen it all.

In 2014, the couple decided to add a completely different company to their business, so Lavinia Good Food was born, a healthy lunchroom in the historic city centre of Amsterdam. In 2017 they opened the second lunchroom at the Amstelveenseweg 192.

As the name suggests, Lavinia Good Food, is all about serving good food. Lavinia's clients are conscious consumers, aware of the environmental impact of their food, and who appreciate fairtrade and locally souced products. With this ethos in mind, the menu at Lavinia centres around fresh, colourful and mostly vegetarian food.

Lavinia serves breakfast and lunch and also offers 'Lavinia All For Yourself'. Lavinia can be reserved for corporate or private parties from 16 guests upwards. This fuss-free option means that the team at Lavinia will serve their food and drinks, and you can just enjoy the evening.

Lavinia constantly innovates and have become known for their creativity in the kitchen. Menus and recipes are constantly tested and presented in new ways. For example all types of pizzetta's, energizing breakfast bowls, and divers lunch dishes. Also popular are the vegan, raw and gluten-free cakes, which have built up a reputation for being truly amazing.

Karel and Sonia are inspired by colour, flavour and wholesome ingredients, and their food is testament to this passion for good cuisine. Everyday a selection of fresh salads are made to look appetisingly beautiful and are just waiting for customers to give them a go!

Lavinia Good Food
VEGGIE MEATBALLS

At Lavinia, it's all about Good Foods. We try to seduce our guests with alternatives to reduce the consumption of meat. Also, we try to promote meat-free meals, without missing out on anything spectacular. On the contrary; our guests are usually surprised when they try our veggie stuff. We LOVE meatballs, and we saw a great opportunity to come up with a veggie version of it. Give it a try and you'll be hooked and the king/queen of the kitchen!

Preparation time: 45 minutes | Cooking time: 45 minutes | Serves 6

Ingredients

125g dried brown lentils, picked over and rinsed

1 bay leaf

500ml vegetable or mushroom broth

224g cremini mushrooms, roughly chopped

60g old-fashioned oats

A pinch of red pepper flakes

2 tbsp olive oil

1 white onion, chopped

3–4 garlic cloves, minced

60g flat-leaf parsley leaves, washed, dried and roughly chopped

60g oregano, roughly chopped

½ tsp thyme, roughly chopped

60ml red wine

2 egg whites (about 70g, omit if making vegan)

Sea salt and freshly ground black pepper

For the bread:

1kg self-raising flour

400g Greek yoghurt

Fleur de sel

To serve:

Mozzarella

Tomato sauce

Fresh basil

Method

Preheat oven to 210°c and line a baking sheet with parchment paper.

Combine the lentils, bay leaf and vegetable broth in a medium saucepan, bring to the boil, then reduce the heat to low and simmer for 10 minutes. The lentils will be a little undercooked, but that's ok! Remove from the heat, drain and let cool for a few minutes. Discard the bay leaf.

In a food processor, combine the mushrooms, oats, lentils and the red pepper flakes. Pulse/blend until the mixture is pretty well pulverized but still a bit chunky, not too smooth.

Heat the olive oil in a large skillet over medium heat, then add the chopped onion and a pinch of sea salt. Cook, stirring often, until the onion is starting to soften and turning golden at the edges, about 5 minutes. Add the garlic and cook, stirring, for about 30 seconds. Stir in lentil-mushroom mixture and cook until browned, about 5 minutes, stirring constantly.

Add the red wine to the skillet and continue to cook, stirring constantly, until the liquid has been absorbed. Remove from the heat and, if you're using a pan that retains heat like cast iron, transfer the mixture to a heat-safe bowl. Season with salt and pepper to taste. Allow the mixture to cool until it is comfortable to handle. When cool, add the freshly chopped parsley, oregano and thyme.

Mix in the eggs whites, if using, to the lentil and mushroom mixture. Use an ice cream scoop to shape the mixture into a halved ball (about 5 cm diameter). Place each "meatball" onto the baking sheet, leaving an inch of space around each one. Bake for 35 minutes, or until golden brown.

At Lavinia Good Food, we serve the these with a Sicilian tomato sauce, buffalo mozzarella, fresh basil and naan bread. To make the bread, mix the flour and yoghurt with a pinch of fleur de sel. Divide the dough into 35g balls, then flatten and grill each bread with a little olive oil. Simply toast some fresh bread if serving to vegans.

Breaking BREAD

For Le Pain Quotidien, bread is so much more than something to sustain you through the day – it is a way of life.

Le Pain Quotidien is a global bakery with local communities at its heart. The eight bakeries in Amsterdam are all unique despite sharing the same philosophy of gathering around communal tables to enjoy the simple pleasure of breaking bread.

Le Pain Quotidien started life when Alain Coumont first opened a bakery in Brussels in 1990. Alain, a young chef, was struggling to find bread that lived up to his childhood memories of the freshly baked rustic loaves made by his family of skilled bakers. The only solution was to open his own bakery that recreated that beloved familiarity – it became a home from home for people searching for that irresistible taste of fresh baking.

The first bakery opened in The Netherlands in 2009, and 2017 has seen the eighth venue opening its doors. Locations include Spuistraat, Nieuwezijds, De Pijp, Oud Zuid and Beethoven, Gelderlandplein and Stadshart. Each individual bakery strives to immerse itself into the community and each store has a long-serving manager who, along with the rest of the team, knows their regular customers by name – and often have their orders ready before they even arrive!

A commitment to using locally-sourced ingredients is important to the philosophy of the company, whose aim is to serve food that is good for the body, the soul and the earth. A plethora of vegan and vegetarian dishes are available on the menu, as Le Pain Quotidien promotes incorporating plant-based food into our daily diets. 'Eat more plants' is one of their mottos – simply look out for the carrot illustrations on the menus.

It isn't all healthy-eating as far as Le Pain Quotidien are concerned – there is always something to indulge in, such as the delicious cheesecake they have shared in this book. For breakfast, they have a reputation for baking the best croissants in Amsterdam, and the French toast is a popular choice as well.

As people enjoy delicious and wholesome food around their sociable communal tables (Gelderlandplein even has a communal table especially for children), it is easy to see why Le Pain Quotidien has become known as a place to enjoy the simplicity of good food and good company.

Le Pain Quotidien
CHILLI SIN CARNE

No one will miss the meat in this dish, and accompaniments like guacamole and sour cream make it easy to adjust to everyone's taste and preferences.

Preparation time: 15 minutes | Cooking time: 20 minutes | Serves 4

Ingredients

2 tbsp extra virgin olive oil

1 carrot, peeled and thinly sliced

2 celery sticks, thinly sliced

2 garlic cloves, chopped

1 sprig of thyme

1 bay leaf

1 tsp smoked paprika

1 tbsp cumin

1 tsp sea salt

200g firm tofu, diced

1 tbsp brown or barley miso

400g canned peeled plum tomatoes

200g red kidney beans, drained

100g white kidney beans, drained

100g canned chickpeas, drained

100g canned sweetcorn, drained

Method

Heat the olive oil in a saucepan, add the carrot, celery, garlic, herbs, spices and salt, and sweat over medium heat for 5 minutes or until the vegetables are softened. Add the tofu and miso. Break up the plum tomatoes, then add them to the pan. Reduce the heat to low, cover and simmer for 10 minutes, stirring occasionally.

Add all the canned beans, the chickpeas and the sweetcorn to the pan. Simmer for another 5 minutes or until the sauce is thick and slightly reduced. Divide the chili sin carne between four bowls and serve with accompaniments of your choice.

NY CHEESECAKE

To remove from the mould, slide the hot, wet blade tip of a knife around the vertical sides of the mould. Turn out carefully and place on a large dish. Decorate with strawberries or raspberries and serve with a red berry coulis or a slightly runny jam or jelly.

Preparation time: 15 minutes | Cooking time: 45 minutes | Serves 12

Ingredients

For the cream:

250g sugar or fructose

50g pastry flour

Pinch of salt

600g cream cheese (Philadelphia, Kiri or Saint Moret for example)

4 eggs

2 egg yolks

1 tsp natural vanilla extract

For the biscuit base:

12 speculoos cookies (available at LPQ), crushed

50g melted butter, tepid

Method

Preheat the oven to 200°c. Mix together the sugar, flour and salt. Sift and put into a mixer with the beater attachment. Add the cream cheese and blend, whisking for 1 minute. Add the whole eggs, the egg yolks and the vanilla. Blend quickly to obtain a smooth and homogenous cream.

Take a high-sided round mould, grease lightly and place a disc of baking paper, cut to fit the size of the mould exactly, inside. Using a spatula, mix the crushed speculoos cookie crumbs with the tepid melted butter. Pour into the mould and press down firmly so that the base is uniformly covered. Pour the cheese cream into the mould.

Bake for 10 minutes, then lower the oven temperature to 140°c and bake for a further 35 minutes. Leave to cool for 30 minutes, then refrigerate for 12 hours, still in the mould.

A taste of Dutch
HISTORY

The past and present come together in a unique celebration of Dutch life in the atmospheric environment of Restaurant Lt. Cornelis.

You know that this is no ordinary eatery as soon as you walk through the doors of this remarkable Dutch restaurant. The historic building is light and airy thanks to the beautiful windows through which light streams into the sophisticated dining room. Situated on Voetboogstraat (which fasinatingly translates as 'crossbow' street), the restaurant embraces the history of its location. This street is where the Schutterij (a voluntary city militia who protected Amsterdam during the 16th and 17th centuries) would practise with their crossbows.

Inside the restaurant the eye is immediately drawn to the famous 'schutterstuk' or militia group portrait by Frans Hals. This painting (the original of which is in the Rijksmuseum) was famously finished by Pieter Codde when Frans became fed up with the long commute to Amsterdam. Amongst others, the painting depicts Lt. Cornelis, after whom this charming restaurant is named.

Just like Dutch art, Dutch cuisine inspires people to visit Amsterdam from all over the world. Since the restaurant opened its doors in March 2016, Restaurant Lt. Cornelis has become known for its passion for classic Dutch cuisine and culinary culture. Inspired by the historic street on which it resides, it takes age-old Dutch dishes and brings them up to date for modern diners.

The food is inspired by the seasons, using local produce from the Dutch land and waters to create impressive chef's menus of three, four or five courses. As well as local fresh ingredients, there are some interesting herbs and spices inspired by The Netherlands' colonial past.

The restaurant takes traditional Dutch dishes and translates them to its fine dining setting. Meals that would once have been hearty and sustaining for hard-working farmers have been reinvented with delicate flavours and creative presentation.

Just like its setting, the food is a harmony of past and present, which come together to create a dining experience like no other.

www.restaurantcornelis.amsterdam

Lt. Cornelis
SALTED HERRING WITH BEETROOT AND APPLE

In Amsterdam, fish stands sell raw herring ('haring'), a soused raw fish with a strong taste. Dutch raw herring is hugely popular in Amsterdam. In Holland, people have been eating raw herring for over 600 years. For foreigners, it might be a bit strange to eat a raw fish that has nothing to do with sushi.

Preparation time: 90 minutes | Cooking time: 60 minutes | Serves 4

Ingredients

For the salted herring:

2 salted herring

For the red beetroot:

2 red beetroot

Coarse salt

For the yellow beetroot:

200ml white wine

400ml vinegar

100g sugar

5g mustard seed

5g salt

3 peppercorns

1 yellow beetroot

For the radishes:

4 radishes

For the apple:

1 Granny Smith apple

100ml lemon brandy

100ml lemon juice

100ml ginger syrup

For the onion:

1 large onion

100ml vinegar

100ml white wine

For the dressing:

30g onion liquid

30g egg white

10g vinegar

1g mustard

Salt and pepper

60g sunflower oil

Method

For the salted herring

Remove the tail from the salted herring, then slice the fillet into three pieces and set aside.

For the red beetroot

Preheat the oven to 150˚c. Take an oven tray and cover the bottom with coarse salt. Place 1 red beetroot on top and roast in the oven until the beetroot is cooked. Remove the skin and cut the beetroot into pieces. Slice the other red beetroot into paper-thin slices and place in ice-cold water.

For the yellow beetroot

Put the white wine, vinegar, sugar, mustard seeds, salt and peppercorns in a pan, stir and bring to the boil. Slice the yellow beetroot into 3mm slices and then punch out rounds using a cutter. Cook the yellow beetroot slices in the sweet and sour liquid until just cooked.

For the radishes

Slice the radishes into 1mm thin slices and place in ice-cold water.

For the apple

Slice the apple into 3mm slices and then punch out rounds using a cutter. Mix the brandy, lemon juice and ginger syrup together in a bowl, add the apple and marinate the apple rounds for a few hours. It is best to vacuum-pack the apple rounds with a little bit of liquid, but you can also simply leave the apple in the liquid for a few hours.

For the onion

Peel and slice the onion. Place the sliced onion in a pan with the vinegar and white wine, and reduce the liquid by one-third. Blitz the mixture in a blender until smooth.

For the dressing

Put all the ingredients except the oil in the blender, and blend while you pour the oil slowly into the blender, just like making a mayonnaise.

To serve

Plate up the roasted beetroot, thinly sliced red beetroot, pickled yellow beetroot, thinly sliced radishes, marinated apples, onion purée and salted herring, add the dressing and serve.

Mosey on down to
MAMOUCHE

This modern take on romantic French dining captures the heart of a mother's home-cooking in its food. With a fusion of exotic flavours, Mamouche demonstrates the Dutch appetite for a new eating culture.

Mamouche (Hebrew for 'my sweetheart'), is the fitting namesake of De Pijp's cosy local restaurant in a small corner of Amsterdam, established back in 2000. In its infancy, it was nothing more than a fun and impromptu venture for owner Nizar Yassine. Since then, it has flourished into a popular Dutch hotspot.

Drawing on his Moroccan heritage, his time working and studying in Paris and his travels around the world, Nizar's cuisine is a marriage of flavours, drawing on North African and European influences. But the real secret behind Nizar's dishes, is that they are motivated by the maternal mother figures who were so prevalent in his culinary upbringing. The essence of several cultures pervades all of his recipes, allowing him to put a unique spin on several cultural classics.

Feel-good, motherly food is the order of the day at Mamouche, and seems to be ingrained in the very fabric of the establishment. For returning customers, the classic menu exhibits tasty Moroccan-inspired food and drink, offering authentic French dining – with a twist.

Their sweet starter known as Bastilla: filo pastry filled with onions, raisins, almonds, and chicken, and topped with sugar and cinnamon, is just a taste of what Mamouche offers every day. All its dishes are based in family recipes and values, particularly in those practised by Nizar's grandmother. Now, his favourite childhood dish: lamb tagine served with sweet potatoes, green beans, and plums, has been a bestseller for fifteen years, and is one of several reasons why many of Mamouche's diners are returning customers.

As a boy, his grandmother encouraged him to eat a different vegetable each day of the week: a practise which is now deeply rooted in the philosophy of his own restaurant. Most of his dishes incorporate vegetables, and dishes such as their popular artichoke salad paired with goat's cheese, beetroot, sweet tomatoes, truffles, and an orange dressing, provide a welcome vegetarian alternative.

The dining room, much like the menu, is a careful blend of the old and the new, with its mahogany-panelled walls, ornate candlesticks, and quirky approach of displaying the restaurant's dishes on wall mirrors. Bare bulbs hang low from the ceiling, but soft candlelight is the restaurant's staple, pairing with the flow of classic French and Arabic music to give the restaurant its tranquil ambiance.

Mamouche

Mamouche
MOROCCAN CHICKEN PASTILLA

A traditional Moroccan dish of festivities par excellence, the Pastilla or puff pastry pie with poultry and almonds, is a real mixture of perfumes, flavours and textures. Its realization certainly requires time and patience, but the result is worth it. The poultry is cooked with onions and spices, part of the sauce completely reduced is reserved for the Pastilla, and the other is used for cooking the eggs. Hulled almonds are golden, crushed, sweetened, and cinnamon-flavoured. All these elements are superimposed then wrapped with Pastilla leaves, and the whole thing is brushed with a mixture of butter and oil, baked, then decorated after the cooking of the icing sugar and cinnamon.

Preparation time: 20 minutes | Cooking time: 2 hours | Serves 4

Ingredients

For the chicken:

2 tbsp olive oil

½ a chicken, cut into pieces

110g Smen (fermented butter)

2 onions, finely chopped

A pinch of ground ginger

A pinch of saffron

1 cinnamon stick

50ml water

Salt and pepper

15g parsley, chopped

1 tbsp coriander, chopped

For the almonds:

250g hulled almonds

50ml of sunflower oil

75g caster sugar

½ tsp cinnamon

For the eggs:

15g butter

5 eggs, beaten

To assemble:

5 sheets of Pastilla filo pastry

25g of butter, melted

Cinnamon, to dust

Icing sugar, to dust

Method

Firstly, heat the oil in a large frying pan. Add the chicken and fry just until the skin is crispy and brown before transferring to a plate.

Add the Smen to the pan to melt, and then add the onions to sauté until soft. Add the spices and fry for a couple more minutes.

Return the chicken to the pan; pour in the water and season to taste. Cover and simmer for 30 minutes, or until the chicken is cooked through and tender. Remove the chicken again and set aside. When it is cool enough to handle, discard the bones. Meanwhile, reduce the cooking liquid by half.

For the almonds

To roast the almonds, place the almonds in a greased baking tray, drizzle with the sunflower oil and bake in the oven for around 20 minutes. Add the cinnamon and caster sugar and run them through a nut grinder or crush them with a rolling pin until coarsely ground. Set aside until ready to assemble.

Add the chicken back into the cooking liquid along with the parsley and coriander and stir. Remove from the heat, remove the cinnamon stick and leave to cool.

For the eggs

In a small frying pan, melt the butter, crack the eggs and scramble them. Set aside until ready to assemble. Make sure the scrambled eggs are not under cooked and runny.

To assemble

Preheat the oven to 180°c and grab a 28cm round ovenproof dish.

Brush a sheet of filo with melted butter. Drape it over the dish, gently pushing it into the corners without tearing it. Repeat with another sheet of filo, placing it at right angles to the first. Repeat with a further 2 sheets of filo, placing them on a diagonal angle.

Place in the filling in this order: a layer of the chicken mixture, a layer scrambled eggs and finally, a layer grinded almonds.

Fold over the overhanging filo, in reverse order – the filling should be just about covered by the filo. Cut the remaining 2 sheets of filo to fit the dish.

Brush with melted butter, then cover the pie with the pastry, tucking under any corners. Bake for 30 minutes, or until crisp and brown.

Leave to cool a little before dusting it with the icing sugar and cinnamon.

Mediterranean
ATMOSPHERE

For a taste of the Mediterranean way of life in the middle of De Pijp, look no further than Oresti's taverna.

Owned by Carin and Orestis, and run with the help of their two daughters Alexia and Litsa, Oresti's taverna is a family-run restaurant where the food, wine and ambience all come together to create the perfect relaxed dining experience.

Orestis simply loves to cook. He learnt to cook from his mother and grandmother at their Greek home in Pireas, a coastal town near Athens. Everything he loves about Greek cuisine – the long, slow dinner times where the whole family gathers round the table to enjoy good food and good wine – he also recognised in other Mediterranean cultures, particularly Spain.

When he opened his restaurant in the lively area of De Pijp with his Dutch partner Carin, he wanted to take all the wonderful elements of those Mediterranean cuisines and bring them together in one place.

Carin and Orestis guarantee the quality of their ingredients by sourcing all of their products carefully. If it can be bought locally, it is. Vegetables are brought in fresh daily from nearby farmers and sustainable fish is sourced from a local supplier. But when it comes to those special ingredients that can only be found abroad, they always look for the best they can. Feta, olives and olive oil are imported from Greece, while top-quality serrano ham and chorizo are sourced from Spain.

Of course, when it comes to Mediterranean cuisine, the wine is just as important as the food! Every year Carin and Orestis travel to vineyards in Europe to taste and select wines for their wine list. In 2016, they worked together with colleagues from different companies in the hospitality business and a vineyard in Spain to blend their own house wine which features the name of the restaurant on the label. You know the wine will be delicious when the owner has put his name to it!

The charm of this cosy restaurant is down to the warm welcome from the family, as well as the great food and wine. A love of hospitality certainly runs in the blood – Orestis and Carin's daughters, Alexia and Litsa, are both studying hospitality and work at the restaurant in the evenings. Customers report that they fall in love with the relaxed atmosphere and Mediterranean-style warmth of this lovely family business as soon as they walk through the doors.

Oresti's taverna also offers the possibility to rent out a room for groups. So you can even celebrate your party or hold your corporate event or meeting!

Oresti's Taverna

Oresti's Taverna
SPANAKOPITA

I got inspired when I tasted the spanakopita at my favourite bakery, Begnis, on the island of Salamina where I spent my younger years. At that time, I said to myself that when I grew up and opened a restaurant, that dish must be on the menu.

Preparation time: 20 minutes | Cooking time: 30 minutes | Serves 10

Ingredients

Olive oil, for cooking

1 onion, chopped

500g wild spinach

100g feta

3g dill

2 eggs

10 puff pastry, sheets

Salt and black pepper

Method

Preheat the oven to 220°c. Heat a little olive oil in a frying pan, add the onion and cook over a low heat until softened. Blanch the spinach and add it to a bowl with the onion. Add the feta, dill, beaten eggs (reserving a little for brushing) and salt and pepper. Mix all the ingredients carefully.

Lay the pastry out and divide the mixture between the sheets. Roll the pastry around the filling and place on a baking sheet lined with baking parchment. Brush with the reserved beaten egg and bake in the preheated oven for about 25-30 minutes, until the pastry is golden brown.

GAMBAS ORESTIS

This meal will bring you to ecstasy with a good piece of bread and a serious glass of white wine.

Preparation time: 10 minutes | Cooking time: 10 minutes | Makes 8

Ingredients

50ml olive oil

8 black tiger prawns, body peeled

½ tsp sambal

1 tsp dried dill

Splash of white wine

100ml cream

Salt

Method

Put a frying pan over a high heat and pour the oil into it. When the oil is hot, lay the prawns in the pan and turn them over. Put a little salt on them but be careful because you will be using sambal which is quite salty too.

While the prawns are turning a nice rose colour put the sambal into the middle of the pan (not on the prawns) and sprinkle the dill over all over the gambas. Finish it off with a splash of wine and the cream. Leave the pan for a little while on the heat and wait for the sauce to get thick before serving.

Flippin' delicious
SINCE 1973

No visit to Amsterdam is complete without sampling a traditional Dutch pancake, and The Pancake Bakery has been famous for serving the best pancakes in town for over 40 years.

Located in a converted warehouse on the Prinsengracht canal, The Pancake Bakery is one of Amsterdam's must-visit foodie gems. The historic building that houses this culinary institution can often only be spotted by the queues of people that form outside at busy times.

It is a family business in the truest sense. It is owned by Bastiaan Schaafsma, who spent the first few years of his life living just upstairs. His parents took on the business in 1980, although it had been running since 1973 before that. When the Schaafsma family took the reins, the restaurant flourished into the much-loved icon it is today. It can proudly claim to be the oldest pancake bakery in the city.

The key to any good pancake is, of course, the batter. Theirs was created by Bastiaan's father and the secret recipe remains a well-kept family secret. Along with traditional Dutch pancakes with sugar or syrup, classic savoury choices like bacon and cheese, and those much-loved favourites such as banana and Nutella, The Pancake Bakery has an international menu. From Indonesian with chicken in peanut sauce and crispy onions to Greek-themed options with lamb gyros, feta and tzatziki, pancakes are the perfect vessels to showcase flavours from around the world.

Although there are a staggering 75 options on the menu in total, the team are always devising new specials. And sometimes a special is simply so popular that the team have no choice but to include it permanently.

Each table is adorned with a bottle of classic Dutch syrup. For Bastiaan, this sweet Dutch topping can transform pancakes from great to incredible. He will often encourage visitors to try it on their bacon and cheese pancakes for a sensational sweet/salty experience.

When asked to sum up what The Pancake Bakery is all about, Bastiaan explains that it is taking something as simple as a pancake and making it into something special. With fresh ingredients and a little love and care, they create delicious meals out of this traditional Dutch dish… or as he puts it: "The recipe is simple, the result divine."

The Pancake Bakery
BACON AND APPLE PANCAKES

For the pancake batter, we have a secret recipe... but you can make your own batter with fresh milk, eggs and flour.

Preparation time: 2 minutes | Cooking time: 5 minutes | Serves 1

Ingredients

1 fresh green apple, such as Granny Smith

3–4 thin slices of bacon

1 portion of pancake batter

Butter, for cooking

Stroop (Dutch syrup), to serve

Method

Peel the fresh green apple, cut it into thin slices and keep them next to you. Heat the pan with some butter so that the pancake won't stick. Add the thin slices of bacon and cook until crispy, then add the slices of apple. Don't let it cook, but immediately add the batter. Pick up the pan and roll out the batter so you will have a nice and thin pancake.

Let the pancake cook for about a minute (that depends on how hot your stovetop is) and then flip the pancake. Cook the other side for about 1–2 minutes. Your pancake is now ready to eat! Don't forget to add a lot of stroop (Dutch syrup) when you eat it!

LEMON AND SUGAR PANCAKES

For our lemon and sugar pancake there is only a little bit of preparation needed.

Preparation time: 2 minutes | Cooking time: 5 minutes | Serves 1

Ingredients

1 portion of pancake batter

1 lemon, quartered

Butter, for cooking and to serve

Icing sugar, for sprinkling

Method

Heat the pan and use some butter so the pancake won't stick. Add the batter, pick up the pan and roll out the batter so you will have a nice and thin pancake again. Let the pancake cook for about a minute (that depends on how hot your stovetop is) and then flip the pancake. Cook the other side until it is done.

Transfer the pancake to the plate and sprinkle it with icing sugar. Take a lemon quarter and stick a fork in it, so you can squeeze the lemon easily. You can use as much lemon as you like. For the finishing touch, you can add some butter to taste. Enjoy your pancake meal!

Singing with your SUPPER

Amsterdam's deliciously different restaurant Pasta e Basta is a treat for all the senses – where singing waitresses and waiters create the most memorable meal.

Located in the Golden Bend of the "Spiegelkwartier", Pasta e Basta has been at the heart of this arty neighbourhood, surrounded by beautiful galleries, art studios and antique stores, since 1995.

It is situated within a historic building that was once a 19th-century bank, and the evidence of its former use is all around – the vaults, pillars and thick, firm walls remain. The bank's safe has been transformed into the dinner bar, where 'startenders' pour glasses of wine and shake up tasty cocktails.

Known for its warm atmosphere and honest hospitality, Pasta e Basta is home to a team of talented, singing waiting staff, every one of whom is a professional singer. Their goal is to amaze guests every night with good service and strong performances. From opera to disco, every member of the team takes a turn to delight the diners.

More than just dinner, a night at Pasta e Basta is an experience to remember – imagine being in a stunning Italian cantina with your loved one, family, friends or business associates, when all of a sudden, a beautiful waitress starts singing an aria, a pop song or part of a musical. Whether it is a romantic dinner for two or a group outing, the Italian-style social element of an evening at Pasta e Basta is what sets it apart as a place for both culinary and cultural enjoyment.

Star chef Ron Blaauw shared his gastronomic expertise to create a wonderful menu together with chef Diederick Landhuis. The kitchen of Pasta e Basta is as Italian as can be, with fresh, rustic and seasonal ingredients at its heart, such as freshly made pasta, seasonal vegetables, free-range meat, sustainable fish, good-quality olive oil and the finest dried pasta. There is a simplicity to the menu, which is inspired by traditional recipes with ingenious twists. As the name says, 'pasta and that's it'!

The meal would not be complete without some tasty Italian wine. Most of the wines are supplied by small family-run Italian wineries, and there are plenty of choices available by the glass.

For a truly unique evening of food and music, Pasta e Basta is one of Amsterdam's special culinary gems.

Pasta e Basta

GREEN SPAGHETTI WITH ZUCCHINI, ASPARAGUS, FRESH SEAFOOD AND PANKO GREMOLATA

This recipe, by D.O.N Landhuis, chef de cuisine at Pasta e Basta Amsterdam, is a beautiful, vibrant pasta dish packed with fresh seafood and zesty flavours.

Preparation time: 10 minutes | Cooking time: 20 minutes | Serves 4

Ingredients

For the panko gremolata:

150g panko breadcrumbs

3 sprigs thyme

3 sprigs rosemary

1 orange, zest

1 lemon, zest

1 lime, zest

2 cloves garlic, grated

Olive oil

For the pasta:

200g cherry tomatoes

500g green spaghetti

4 shallots

150ml olive oil

6 garlic gloves, finely chopped

1 red chilli, finely chopped, plus extra to serve (optional)

250g zucchini spaghetti

2 lemons, juice

1 lemon, zest

8 scallops

8 prawns, peeled and cut in half

200g asparagus, chopped

500g clams

White wine

Salt and pepper

Basil leaves, to garnish

Method

For the panko gremolata

Mix all the ingredients for the panko gremolata and pan fry until golden brown. Remove from the pan and place on to a kitchen towel to drain the excess oil. Set aside for garnishing.

For the pasta

Preheat the oven to 180°c. Put the cherry tomatoes in an oven tray and roast in the preheated oven for 6 minutes. Bring a large pan of salted water to the boil. Cook the fresh green spaghetti according to the package instructions or until al dente. Drain well. Sauté the shallots in a little of the oil and fry until translucent, then add the garlic and chilli. Fry these ingredients together briefly and then add the zucchini spaghetti. Finally add the lemon juice.

Mix the cooked green spaghetti in with your zucchini pasta and flavour to taste with salt, pepper and lemon zest. Heat the remaining oil in a frying pan and fry the scallops until golden brown on each side. Place the scallops on the roasted cherry tomato platter. Add the prawns to the pan and fry quickly with the chopped asparagus. Then add the clams and deglaze with a little white wine. Cover with a lid and let the clams cook until their shells open, 1–2 minutes.

To serve

Place the spaghetti mixture in the centre of the dish. Divide the seafood and asparagus on top of the pasta. Garnish with the roasted cherry tomatoes, panko gremolata and basil leaves. For extra spice, roughly chop up some chilli or add some freshly ground black pepper.

Buon apetito!

Time to RELAX

For an escape from the hustle and bustle of the city, there is nowhere that offers such a peaceful dining experience like Pont 13.

Pont 13 is an authentic ferry that dates back to 1927. Today it has been lovingly converted into a unique waterfront restaurant. More than simply a place to dine, Pont 13 has created a reputation as the best place to truly escape the crowds and enjoy a few hours of serenity.

In fact, for many, being on-board Pont 13 is almost like being on holiday. Close your eyes for a few moments and enjoy the wind whistling past your ears and feel the gentle movement of the water beneath you. The terrace is the perfect place to enjoy a cold beer while the sun shines on your face and you watch the boats sailing peacefully past – a few hours of utter relaxation before heading back into the city feeling replenished.

As you would expect in a waterside eatery, the fresh fish is extremely popular. Like the meat, it is cooked on a charcoal grill, which gives it extra flavour. The food is served by a friendly team who always make sure to have a smile on their faces.

This creates a wonderfully relaxed setting where customers can enjoy their food and drinks in unique surroundings.

Unfortunately, Amsterdam isn't blessed with sunshine every day, so luckily the interior of the boat is just as characterful as the terrace. During the renovation, the team were careful to keep the industrial character of the boat, retaining many original features from the ferry.

The old engine room is reserved for hiring out for meetings or presentations – what a unique place to gather a group of colleagues together! For larger groups or parties, the entire restaurant can be hired out exclusively. It has become a popular spot for weddings, too, as it is an official wedding location. A wedding ceremony, dinner and evening party can be arranged for up to 150 guests, which would certainly be a wedding to remember forever.

One more thing that sets Pont 13 out as something a little out of the ordinary… guests can rent boats for a little trip on the water. What a perfect way to start the evening.

Pont 13
CHEESECAKE OF WHITE CHOCOLATE AND YOGHURT

This simple cheesecake is luxurious thanks to the creamy white chocolate. It needs to set in the fridge for 8 hours before serving, so it is best to start this early in the day.

Preparation time: 8 hours 30 minutes | Serves 8-10

Ingredients

65g butter, melted

130g Bastogne biscuits, crushed to a powder

250ml cream

4 pieces of gelatine (7g)

200g white chocolate, cut into small chunks

55g sugar

400g cream cheese

250ml yoghurt

Tarragon leaves and strawberries, to serve

Method

First mix the melted butter and the Bastogne biscuits together in a food mixer to create a crumble mixture. Cover the bottom of a 25cm spring-form cake pan with this mixture and create an equal layer. Set aside.

Put the cream in a pan over the heat. When it's boiling, turn off the heat and add the gelatine, 150g of the white chocolate and the sugar.

Mix the cream cheese and yoghurt together until smooth. Now, mix the cream mixture together with the cream cheese and yoghurt mixture. Allow it to cool down, stirring until it becomes thicker.

Gently pour the mixture into the pan over the biscuit base. Place it in the fridge to cool down for 30 minutes. After 30 minutes, sprinkle the remaining 50g of white chocolate on top to finish. Leave the cheesecake to set in the fridge for at least 8 hours before serving.

To serve

Serve the cheesecake with tarragon leaves and strawberries.

One of a KIND

Dining in the first commercial broadcast station of The Netherlands is a totally unique experience – step inside REM Eiland Restaurant.

Walk into REM Eiland Restaurant and you are stepping into Dutch history. Today it is a popular dining spot, but the previous function of REM Eiland was another type of ground-breaking social pleasure – it was the home of the first commercial broadcast station.

TV Noordzee caused a sensation when it began airing entertainment to millions of viewers – a rebel group of pirates who were broadcasting from the North Sea. This unique channel created a stir across the country and older people will remember bouncing around in anticipation while their father clambered onto the roof to install the aerial and their mother whipped up some food to accompany the exciting broadcast.

Although it was incredibly popular, the Dutch government adopted the anti-REM law in an effort to shut it down. And on 17 December 1964 at exactly 9am, an invasion of police helicopters and boats marked the end of this famous station.

So, what has become of it today? It has been transformed into a modern restaurant that showcases its unique history by keeping many of its original features alive. Look around and you will see that you are dining on the former helicopter deck – not many restaurants can make that claim!

If the unique history that surrounds the diner isn't enough, there is also the addition of the incredible view. By locating the station at the Houthavens of Amsterdam, it has created a breath-taking perspective that provides the perfect background for an unusual lunch or dinner.

Whatever you choose from the varied menu, you will be enjoying so much more than just a delicious meal – you will be experiencing a piece of Dutch national history.

REM Eiland
SOUFFLE OF OLD AMSTERDAM

The rich flavour of Old Amsterdam cheese is paired with luxurious truffle tapenade in this delicious soufflé.

Preparation time: 5 minutes | Cooking time: 30 minutes | Serves 8

Ingredients

120g butter

120g flour

1 litre milk

80g truffle tapenade

320g Old Amsterdam cheese, grated

120g Parmesan cheese, grated

12 egg yolks (300g)

12 egg whites (360g)

Salt and pepper

Method

Preheat the oven to 170°c. Melt the butter in a pan and let it sizzle for a bit. Add the flour and stir through until the mixture becomes dry. Add the milk while stirring and let it become a smooth roux. Now add the truffle tapenade and both of the cheeses to the roux. When the cheese has completely melted into the mixture, take your pan of the stove and let it cool down for a bit. When the mixture is below 40°c, add the egg yolks and gently stir them through.

Whisk the egg whites in a separate bowl until stiff. Now stir the egg whites through the other mixture, making sure it is properly mixed. Season with some salt and pepper.

Put the mixture in a piping bag and fill up little baking moulds to the edge (use silicon muffin sized moulds/cups). Put the moulds in an oven tray, then fill the tray with water so that it comes halfway up the moulds. Put the tray in the preheated oven to bake the soufflés in the bain-marie for about 18 minutes.

Take them out of the oven, remove the moulds from the tray and let them rest on your kitchen counter until the soufflés are back to room temperature. Then place the soufflés in the fridge for about an hour.

To serve

Preheat the oven to 180°c. Take the soufflés out of the fridge and gently remove them from the moulds. Warm up the soufflés on grease proof paper in the preheated oven for 7 minutes.

Ancient CRAFT

The story of The Stillery combines a passion for ancient arts with cutting-edge contemporary science, along with a touch of irrepressible human curiosity...

Today Pascal is the Master Distiller at The Stillery, where he oversees the distillation of their hand-crafted batch-distilled vodka, The Stillery's First. However, Pascal didn't become a Master Distiller overnight – in fact he spent seven years hidden away in the privacy of his attic learning the secrets of this ancient craft.

It was during this period, when Pascal was developing his unique vodka made from dinklewheat (you may know this as spelt), that he began assembling what would eventually become The Stillery's team. He bumped into an old friend, Robin, and shared a few bottles with him. Robin loved it and knew immediately that there would be a market for this hand-crafted spirit.

In 2015 Robin and Pascal formed The Stillery, joined shortly after by the third member of the team, Daan, in 2016. Robin's background in design and engineering allowed him to create a unique brand with simple packaging that reflects the modern-yet-ancient product inside. So, with Robin responsible for the bottle, Pascal (whose background is in molecular biology) responsible for what goes into the bottle, entrepreneur Daan has the task of taking this labour of love to the people of The Netherlands... and further afield.

A dusty attic is no place to be distilling high-quality spirits, so The Stillery moved to a small distillery close to Amsterdam, where the team were lucky enough to make the acquaintance of Arthur and his copper still. Arthur has been a tremendous supporter and champion of The Stillery – letting them use his copper still and being tolerant of their endless experiments!

Having visited many distilleries (and finding the distilling community endlessly welcoming) and learning various techniques, the team have tried practically every method in the book – and a few extra besides. They've experimented with un-malted wheat, oats and rye, and have tried a variety of different yeasts to get to the recipe they have today.

Although dinklewheat vodka is their starting point, their ambitions are much bigger than this single spirit. They launched a limited-edition vodka in 2016 that had been aged in oak, and they have also experimented with herbal spirits, dabbled in gin and even tried an infamous absinthe recipe that dates back to the 19th century.

With such a young, dynamic team driving this new business, they are creating quite a stir in the craft spirit industry of The Netherlands – and customers will be eagerly awaiting these exciting new products to hit the market.

The Stillery
THE MOKUM MULE

Mokum translates as "Amsterdam" in the local Yiddish dialect. It means "home"
or "save haven" and affectionately designates the Dutch capital as the place
to rest your head… but not after you've had our Mokum Mule. This ginger-
inspired feast of perfection is the Dutch answer to the popular Moscow Mule.
This was chosen as 2017's drink of the year by Het Parool.

Preparation time: 5 minutes | Makes 1

Ingredients

A generous amount of ice

40ml The Stillery's First
Dinklewheat Vodka

175ml Fever Tree Ginger Ale

A dash of The Fee Brothers Black
Walnut Cocktail Bitters

Fresh mint, to garnish

Method

Start by filling up a large glass with a generous amount of ice, because the drink needs to
be cold. Add The Stillery's First Dinklewheat Vodka to the glass and top up the drink with
the Fever Tree Ginger Ale.

Our batch-distilled vodka is naturally sweet because we use dinklewheat to make it. The
dinklewheat, or spelt, gives this spirit an interesting almond taste. To enhance these sweet
notes, we add a dash of black walnut cocktail bitters to the mix. Be sure not to overdo it,
most cocktail bitters are naturally quite potent. Garnish with fresh mint and serve.

Have the Thai of YOUR LIFE

The owners of the Thai Food Cafe are taking Amsterdam by storm, one café at a time, serving up enriched Thai dishes in contemporary surroundings.

Nestled in the hum of Amsterdam's historic streets, Thai Food Cafe is the prodigy of owners Melle Schellekens & Ferdinand van de Koppel, together with dedicated influencer and supplier of Thai and Asian cuisine, Mr. Woest. Launched in July 2016, the café has already been named one of the Netherlands' best Thai restaurants, proud to offer up a unique take on Thai cuisine for street food prices.

It all began with a profound passion for Thailand and its intrinsic culture of street food. Thai Food Cafe has now condensed that concept into an edgy, modern space, complete with contemporary décor and a wealth of authentic recipes. Between the leafy green vines spilling from the ceiling, and the rustic, exposed walls which contrast with the brightly-coloured furniture and strung-up twinkle lights, it's difficult not to feel that the Thai Food Cafe is a small seed of Thailand which is fast blossoming in the heart of Amsterdam.

Part of what keeps their menu fresh and enticing, is the keen collaboration between the owners and their farmers back in Thailand. They regularly bring back new and inventive dishes with which to adorn their menu, allowing them to remain versatile within an ever-competitive culinary landscape.

One of their most popular dishes is the Thai Platter, offering a selection of bites, from a traditional lemon grass satay and Chiang Mai sausage, to marinated pork belly and Thai meatballs served with tomato chutney, peanut sauce, and Thai chilli sauce. Most of their dishes are vegetarian-based and gluten-free to advocate healthy, wholesome, feel-good food for everyone.

As well as making it their mission to reimagine Thai street food, they are also eager to pioneer new ways of preserving the purity of their ingredients. Flash-freezing is just one of the ways they're able to lock in the vitamins and minerals already saturating their fresh produce, allowing them to supply food that isn't just visually vibrant, but also a treat for the taste buds.

An in-house karaoke room serves to bring music and laughter into the soul of the establishment, and the café itself appears to run on the publics' schedule, offering quick bites, family meals, a little something to takeaway, or even late evening meals to allow workers to relax after a hard day's work. The Thai Food Cafe is all that's good and appetising about Thai food; it just happens to be singing Thailand's praises on another continent.

Thai Food Cafe
VEGAN PAD THAI

Authentic Pad Thai for vegetarian and vegan Thai food lovers, or those who want a lighter noodle dish without the meat. This Pad Thai recipe offers lots of protein in the form of eggs (or soft tofu for vegans), and ground nuts. And because it's made with rice noodles, Pad Thai can also be made gluten-free. Although vegetables are not strictly part of traditional Pad Thai, I've added some bok choy which tastes yummy with the noodles and makes this dish even more nutritious. Try it - you'll love it!

Preparation time: 20 minutes | Cooking time: 5 minutes | Serves 2

Ingredients

250g dried Pad Thai rice noodles

60ml oil

4 garlic cloves, minced

120g onions, diced

3-4 heads of baby bok choy

45ml vegetable stock or white wine

1-2 eggs (vegans can substitute this for 60g soft tofu)

90g beansprouts

2 spring onions, sliced

30g unsalted dry-roasted peanuts or cashews, chopped

40g fresh coriander or cilantro

Lime wedges

For the Pad Thai sauce:

160g tamarind paste

60ml vegetable or faux chicken stock

50ml soy sauce or wheat-free soy sauce

15ml chilli sauce or 1 tsp chilli flakes

35g brown sugar

Method

Bring a pot of water to boil over a high heat before dunking in the rice noodles and stirring with a fork to separate. Cook for 4-6 minutes, just until the noodles are limp but still too firm to eat (a little firmer than al dente). Noodles should be undercooked at this stage in order to come out right when they are stir-fried. Drain and rinse with cold water.

Combine the Pad Thai sauce ingredients in a bowl, stirring well to dissolve the sugar and tamarind. Note that this sauce should have a very strong-tasting flavour: sweet and sour at first, followed by salty and spicy. Add more sugar if too sour, then set aside.

Warm a wok or large frying pan over a medium-high heat. Add 1-2 tablespoons of oil plus the garlic and onion, then stir-fry for 1 minute to release the fragrance.

Add the bok choy plus enough stock or white wine to keep the ingredients frying nicely. Stir-fry for a further 2 minutes, or until the bok choy is bright green and slightly softened.

Push the ingredients aside and add half a tablespoon of more oil to the centre of the wok/pan. Then add the egg (if using) and briefly scramble.

Add the drained noodles and a third of the sauce. Mix everything together for 1-2 minutes using 2 utensils and a gentle tossing motion (like tossing a salad). Keep the heat between medium-high and high, reducing if noodles begin to stick or burn. Keep adding sauce and continue stir-frying for 3-6 more minutes, or until all the sauce is added and the noodles are soft but still chewy and deliciously sticky. If using soft tofu instead of egg: add this along with the last of the pad Thai sauce. It will break up into small bits and be distributed throughout the dish, just as egg would.

Switch off the heat and add the beansprouts, spring onion and the majority of the nuts. Toss and do a taste-test, adding more soy sauce for more salt/flavour. If too salty or sweet for your taste, add a good squeeze of lime juice. If too sour, add a little more sugar.

To serve, scoop noodles onto a serving platter. Sprinkle with the remaining ground nuts and fresh coriander. Add wedges of fresh-cut lime on the side to be squeezed over just before eating.

A breath of
FRESH AIR

With a bustling street on one side and peaceful green space on the other, De Veranda provides the perfect space to step out of the busy city for a few moments of relaxation.

De Veranda takes its name from its unique setting on the edge of Amsterdam Forest. A veranda is a place that sits on the boundary between the busy inside and the quiet outside – a place to take a break from the hustle and bustle and enjoy a few moments of calm. De Veranda embodies this feeling, nestled between a busy road and the tranquillity of the city forest. It is a place where there is always something going on, but where people can relax, too.

Seven days a week people come here to enjoy the light, bright, contemporary setting. Business meetings take place over lunch, families enjoy the relaxed atmosphere and people come together to sample the globally inspired cuisine.

Since De Veranda opened in 1999 it has become renowned for quality. Maintaining a reputation for high standards over 18 years is no mean feat. Their success is testament to their ambition to offer something a little bit different to the Amsterdam dining scene.

The food can often exceed the expectations of customers, who are blown away by the quality of cuisine on offer in this relaxed eatery. The kitchen takes local ingredients and transforms them into internationally inspired dishes. They make almost everything from scratch on site – if they can't make it themselves, they source it from the best people locally. The bread, for example, comes from one of the city's best bakers.

Flavour is at the forefront of the menu. One of the most popular choices is the slow-cooked Black Angus brisket, which is finished in the charcoal oven to give it a little extra oomph. Served in a sandwich with coleslaw, Gruyère and relish, the meat melts in the mouth thanks to its 10-hour cooking time. Another firm favourite is the Hawaii-inspired Poké bowl, which bursts with flavour from salmon, soya dressing, sesame, noodles and wakame.

The kitchen has a bright and happy atmosphere, and this enables them to consistently produce the type of food that makes mouths water – comforting, delicious and satisfying.

De Veranda

De Veranda
STUFFED FREE-RANGE CHICKEN FROM THE BBQ WITH ZA'ATAR AND HASSELBACK POTATO

You will need two skewers and some twine to tie the stuffed chickens for cooking. The chickens are finished on a BBQ, which gives it a delicious flavour.

Preparation time: 30 minutes | Cooking time: 1 hour | Serves 2

Ingredients

For the chicken:

100g mushrooms

1 tsp garlic, crushed

1 tsp tarragon, chopped

50g chicken livers

100g minced chicken

2 egg whites

50g butter

1 tbsp za'atar

2 large green cabbage leaves

2 free-range chickens, deboned (ask your supplier)

Salt and pepper

Sunflower oil

For the Hasselback potatoes:

2 medium Nicola potatoes, with skins

Oil

Salt

Butter

For the vegetables:

2 yellow beetroots

2 Chioggia beetroots

6 small carrots

2 string beans

6 thyme sprigs

4 garlic sprigs

Salt and pepper

Method

For the chicken

Cut the mushrooms and chop them finely in a food processor until they have a fairly coarse texture. Transfer to a frying pan and fry the mushrooms with the crushed garlic pulp into a dry duxelles. Season with salt and pepper, add the tarragon and cool.

Blitz the chicken livers in the food processor until it is completely smooth, then press through a sieve with the back of a spoon into a bowl. Add the minced chicken to the strained chicken liver, then add the duxelles and the egg whites. Place it all back in the food processor, and blitz until combined. Melt the butter in a small pan and add the za'atar. Cut the stem from both green cabbage leaves and cut into strips about 2cm thick. Add to the butter and za'atar and cook until al dente. Let cool.

Preheat the oven to 140°c and light a charcoal barbecue. Place the boned chickens onto a cutting board with the meat facing up. Spread the stuffing in the shape of a heart onto the chickens, then add the green cabbage in the centre. Fold the sides in, just over one another. Insert the skewer into one end and then zig-zag it through the skin until it is closed. Turn the chickens over and bring them into shape, then tie with twine under the wings and around the legs. Coat the chickens in the remaining za'atar butter, place in the preheated oven and cook for 25 minutes. Let the chickens rest for 15 minutes. Finish the chicken on the barbecue before serving (for 5 minutes in 200°c heat), until golden brown.

For the Hasselback potatoes

Preheat the oven to 200°c. Put a washed potato in a large serving spoon and cut thin slices in the potato, not all the way through. The slices should be 4mm apart. Repeat with the other potato. Place the potatoes on baking paper on a baking sheet, coat with oil and salt, and cook until golden and crispy, approximately 35 minutes. Just before they are ready, remove from the oven and brush with butter.

For the vegetables

Preheat the oven to 200°c. Wash both kinds of beetroot and cook them (skin on) until they are a little bit past al dente. Cut them into wedges. Peel and wash the carrots, then cook until al dente in boiling salted water and drain. Cook the string beans in boiling salted water until al dente, then drain. Mix all of the vegetables together with a bit of oil, the thyme sprigs and cloves of garlic. Season with salt and pepper, then roast in the preheated oven for 5 minutes before serving.

To serve

Serve the chicken from the BBQ with the Hasselback potatoes and roasted vegetables.

Living
LA VIDA

For a little bit of Spanish hospitality, look no further than Vida's freshly cooked tapas and friendly customer service.

Vida Cerveceria and Taperia started life on the 14 February 2013 in a town called Hilversum. The idea was to create a taste of Spain through Spanish-inspired tapas, with influences of the Middle East, Africa and the Pacific, too. Fresh fish, great cuts of meat and seasonal vegetables made up a menu that changes every three months.

From its origin in Hilversum, the team developed their concept and made a lot of friends along the way. The result? A popular hangout that was always crowded with guests. They built on this success by opening a second restaurant in Amsterdam Zuid, in a neighborhood full of expats, locals and tourists. From day one, they amassed a huge variety of customers… young children with their parents, couples having a romantic night out, friends laughing at old memories, businessmen off-duty, tourists from all over the world, and many more. They all came with just one idea, to have a good night out and eat some proper tapas.

Part of their success is down to the knowledgeable staff – they are trained to know every single wine and dish on the menu, as well as knowing the Vida philosophy inside out. Customer service is paramount for the team, who are always happy to stop for a chat with customers, asking them about their day at work or their sightseeing plans, perhaps. Personal service, proper knowledge about their products and real human contact is what they stand for – and what they will always stand for.

Along with a delicious menu, they are proud to serve their own specially brewed IPA. Called Nules, a Spanish Mandarin variety, they brewed it in collaboration with Jopen Brewery in Haarlem. This is just one way that they strive to offer something a little different in their restaurant, appreciating how people are always looking for new discoveries when it comes to food and drink.

Walking in the doors at Vida, the smell of fresh garlic, grilled meat and Spanish pepper welcomes you. You can see the cooks working in the half-open kitchen. You hear people laughing, toasting glasses and sharing tapas. Take a seat at a table or the bar and enjoy a little taste of Spain in Amsterdam. This is life. This is Vida!

Vida
PULPO HORNEADO

We call the broth for this delicious octopus dish WUPS. This is Dutch for Wortel (carrot), Ui (onion), Prei (leek) and Selderij (celery).

Preparation time: 15 minutes | Cooking time: 1 hour 15 minutes | Serves 3

Ingredients

1 large carrot, washed and sliced in big pieces

½ bunch of celery, washed and sliced

1 leek, washed and sliced, white part only

1 big white onion, peeled and sliced

3 garlic, cloves, bruised, plus extra to finish

3 bay leaves

90ml tomato paste

100ml white whine

1 whole octopus (2-3 kg)

Salt, to taste

Olive oil, for cooking

Spanish red pepper, sliced, to serve

Chives, chopped, to serve

Lemon wedges, to serve

Method

Place a big cooking pot on the stove over a high heat. Heat some good-quality olive oil in the pan, then add the carrot, celery, leek and onion and cook these briefly. Add the garlic and bay leaves and mix this in the cooking pot. Cook briefly then add the tomato paste and cook for 3 minutes.

Deglaze the pan with the white wine, then add enough water to make sure that all the ingredients are under water. Bring this all to the boil and dip the octopus into the liquid three times; each time for 1 minute in the broth, with intervals of 2 minutes in between.

After the third interval of 2 minutes, leave the octopus in the pan and cook for 1 hour over low heat. After an hour, take out the octopus and let it cool down.

When the octopus has cooled down completely, you can cut the tentacles into pieces. Cut off the tentacle as close as possible to the head. Slice the tentacles in pieces of approximately 1cm.

To serve

Heat some good-quality olive oil in a flat cooking pan over a high heat. When the oil is screaming hot, add some pieces of the tentacle, combined with some small pieces of fresh garlic and two slices of Spanish red pepper. Give the tentacle a good touch in the hot oil. Make sure the outside has a nice bite. Serve the tentacle pieces on a plate and garnish it with some freshly chopped chive and a wedge of fresh lemon. ¡Buen Provecho!

Tips

Make sure the raw octopus doesn't stick to itself when you add it to the broth. This prevents you from having uneven cooked pieces. Give the octopus a good shake to loosen it all up!

Stay sharp on the cooking time of the octopus, this is really crucial. If you're not strict enough on this, your octopus could become tough.

You can use the broth twice to prepare the octopus.

Wild about PIES

The only place to sample New Zealand-style savoury meat pies in Amsterdam, Wild Moa Pies has built up a loyal following for its irresistible meat and veggie pies.

Wild Moa Pies is the brainchild of Monique Koorn, who has combined her love for food and her passion for New Zealand into this popular pie spot. Monique has been a chef since 1982 and worked in The Netherlands before moving to New Zealand in 1988. Her love of Antipodean culture resulted in an action-packed few years working within the food industry and outdoor activities – she racked up 53 bungy jumps while working at the Auckland Climbing Centre, taught cookery skills to young people at a training centre and worked in onsite catering for films and commercials.

Her appreciation of food is as diverse and wide-ranging as her zest for life, and she has taught workshops on cuisines from French, Greek and Italian to Japanese, South American and Indian, as well as more unusual subjects like survival cooking.

This love of international cuisine shines through in Wild Moa Pies, which she started in 2001. Named after the extinct flightless bird, the moa, which was native to New Zealand, Wild Moa Pies embodies the love that Monique has for her adopted home. From hangi to hongi, she could teach many a New Zealand native a thing or two about Kiwi culture. She has fried up paua and pippies in a hubcap, taken part in many a sausage sizzle and has a staggering 15 barbecues in her collection!

She actually began the business by importing sauces and condiments from New Zealand and Australia, such as Kaitaia Fire and Waha Wera – the pies were simply to go with them. However, the pies were simply too delicious to be a sideline, and they were soon the star of the show! The secret to Monique's famous pies lies in the puff pastry crust, which is crisp and delicious. The crust encases a variety of fillings – try classic chicken or steak pie, opt for bacon and egg or spinach and feta, or see what the 'pie of the day' is when you arrive. Wild Moa Pies is very much a 'green' business, with all deliveries being made by bicycle.

While you are at Wild Moa Pies, you can also stock up on those antipodean delights (think Tim Tams or Vegemite!) that are essential to any Kiwi or Aussie while away from home. They are also popular with many Dutch people, who, like Monique, fell in love with the way of life across the globe on their travels, and like to keep a little taste of Australia or New Zealand back home in Amsterdam.

Wild Moa Pies

AWESOME LENTIL AND AUBERGINE PIE

Well I am not a lentil fan to be honest... but this pie is so popular I have to comply! The nice thing about it is that the filling itself is vegan, and although I like to use all-butter pastry, you could choose a vegan pastry instead.

Preparation time: 15 minutes | Cooking time: 45 minutes | Serves 16

Ingredients

4 tins of lentils (or 1kg black lentils cooked according to packet instructions)

6 tablespoons olive oil

2 aubergines, large

Vegetable stock, for steaming the aubergine

4 white onions, finely chopped

3 tbsp freshly chopped thyme

4-6 garlic cloves, to taste, finely chopped

2 red peppers, chopped into small pieces

2 red chilli peppers, finely chopped

A bunch of parsley, chopped

1 tbsp cumin

Salt and pepper

1 lemon, zest and juice

1 bunch of spring onions, sliced into small rings

4 packs of all-butter pastry (or make your own using 1kg flour)

Method

Preheat the oven to 225°c.

Drain the tinned lentils (or cook and drain the dried lentils). Chop the aubergines into 5mm cubes.

Heat a little of the olive oil in a frying pan and fry the aubergines with a little salt and pepper. Add a little vegetable stock to speed up the cooking. Once cooked, remove the aubergines from the pan and set aside.

Add a little more oil to the pan and add the finely chopped onions. Fry with the thyme and half of the garlic until softened, then remove from the pan and set aside.

Add a little more oil to the pan and add the red peppers and chilli peppers. Fry until cooked, and then add the aubergines and onions back into the pan, along with the lentils, the remaining garlic, parsley, cumin, lemon zest and juice, and sliced spring onions.

Roll out the pastry on a flour-dusted surface. Line 16 individual pie tins with the pastry, saving enough pastry to make the lids. Fill the pastry cases with the filling and then top with a pastry lid. Seal the edges and decorate the top of the pie so that you know what filling is inside it.

Bake in the preheated oven for 25 minutes until the pastry is golden. Check the bottom of the pastry, it should be crisp and delicious!

The DIRECTORY

These great businesses have supported the making of this book; please support and enjoy them.

ATL Seafood
Loggerstraat 55
1976 CX, Ijmuiden
Telephone: +31(0) 255 525 536
Website: www.atlseafood.nl.
Our mission is to deliver the best fish to restaurants, hotels and catering.

Bao Buns
Telephone: +31(0) 62 601 68 09
Website: www.justinbrownchef.com/bao-buns
A pop-up street food concept serving homemade bao buns, ramen, Taiwanese and Korean cuisine in different locations in Amsterdam. Check the website to find out where Bao Buns is popping up next.

Restaurant Blauw Amsterdam
Amstelveenseweg 158-160
1075 XN Amsterdam
Telephone: +31(0) 20 675 50 00
Website: www.restaurantblauw.nl
We invite you to enjoy the enormous diversity of the Indonesian kitchen in a warm, modern setting.

THE BUTCHER Albert Cuyp
Albert Cuypstraat 129
1072 CS Amsterdam
Telephone: +31(0) 20 470 78 75
Website www.the-butcher.com
THE BUTCHER Albert Cuypstraat is open from 11am until after midnight, making it the ideal spot for a delicious burger; whether you crave a late breakfast, tasty lunch, hearty dinner or midnight snack.

THE BUTCHER Social Club
A'DAM Toren, Overhoeksplein 1
1031 KS Amsterdam
Telephone: +31(0) 20 215 95 15
Website: www.the-butcher.com/socialclub
THE BUTCHER Social Club fuses a famous burger joint with a laid-back lounge, vintage video games hall and social hub with an eclectic events programme featuring live gigs, sports screenings, terrace parties and so much more – and it's open 24/7 on weekends.

THE BUTCHER West
Foodhallen, Bellamyplein 51
1053 AT Amsterdam
Website www.the-butcher.com
It's the signature sauces, the freshest selection of herbs and – of course – the prime Aberdeen Angus beef that combines to make THE BUTCHER burgers consistently voted the best in Amsterdam – and THE BUTCHER's Foodhallen outpost offers the same signature menu of burgers as its other locations across the city.

Café Caron
Frans Halsstraat 28 H
Amsterdam
1072 BS
Telephone: +31(0) 20 675 86 68
Website: www.cafecaron.nl
Rich French cuisine in its simplicity: where the atmosphere is relaxed, the food tastes good and the wine flows generously.

Café AMOI

Kinkerstraat 53

1053 DE Amsterdam

Telephone: +31(0) 20 846 27 55

Website: www.cafeamoi.nl

A modern Indonesian eatery who doesn't do things the old-fashioned way.

Café Loetje

Johannes Vermeerstraat 52

1071 DT Amsterdam

Telephone: +31(0) 20 66 28 173

Website: www.loetje.com

In this restaurant lie the roots of the Loetje concept; this is where our sirloin steak was successfully put on the menu in the 70s and – as it turned out – became the basis for all the other Loetje establishments in the Netherlands.

Loetje Centraal

Stationsplein 10

1012 AB Amsterdam

Telephone: +31(0) 20 62 33 777

Website: www.loetje.com

The restaurant, located in a beautiful historic building, right in the heart of Amsterdam on the water, is bright, spacious and homely inside, with a lot of typical Dutch and Delft blue elements incorporated in the interior.

The Chippy

Telephone: +31(0) 62 601 68 09

Website: www.thechippy.nl

Traditional fish and chips, to eat in or takeaway in Amsterdam – the location changes weekly, so check the website to find out where The Chippy is popping up next.

De Drie Graefjes

Rokin 128-130

1012 LD Amsterdam

Eggertstraat 1

1012 NN Amsterdam

Telephone: +31(0) 20 627 47 61

Website: www.dedriegraefjes.com

Lunchroom, high tea and American bakery.

The Duchess

Spuistraat 172

1012 VT Amsterdam

Telephone: +31(0) 20 811 33 22

Website: www.the-duchess.com

THE DUCHESS restaurant, bar and tea lounge resides in one of Amsterdam's best-kept historic gems, the grand former KAS Bank, where an elegant menu of nouveau-Nicoise cuisine is served alongside award-winning cocktails and a refined afternoon tea.

Grizzly American Restaurant & Bar

Warmoesstraat 64

1012 JH Amsterdam

Telephone: +31(0) 20 221 44 32

Website: www.grizzly-amsterdam.nl

American restaurant and bar offering a range of delicious American cuisine, special beers and fine wines.

The Harbour Club Amsterdam Oost

Cruquiusweg 67

1019 AT Amsterdam

Telephone: +31(0) 20 767 04 21

The Harbour Club Amsterdam Zuid

Apollolaan 2

1077 BA Amsterdam

Nederland

Telephone: +31(0) 20 570 57 31

Website: www.theharbourclub.com

A unique location in Amsterdam with international allure, a vibrant atmosphere and extraordinarily great food

Herengracht Restaurant & Bar

Herengracht 435

1017 BR Amsterdam

Telephone: +31(0) 20 616 24 82

Website: www.deherengracht.com

Restaurant and bar with a prime location on the Herengracht canal, featuring a unique terrace and garden during the summer months.

Het Warenhuis

Haarlemmerstraat 65

1013 EL Amsterdam

Telephone: +31(0) 20 792 00 11

Website: www.hetwarenhuis. amsterdam

Seated behind the immense window lounging on the stretched sofa or working at one of the shared tables, Amsterdam meets, drinks and dates at HET WARENHUIS at the Haarlemmerstraat.

Hotel Die Port Van Cleve

Nieuwezijds Voorburgwal 176-180

1012 SJ Amsterdam

Telephone: +3120 714 20 00

Website: www.dieportvancleve.com

Historic hotel and brasserie, serving their famous numbered steaks for over 100 years.

IZAKAYA Asian Kitchen & Bar

Albert Cuypstraat 2-6

1072 CT Amsterdam

Telephone: +31(0) 20 305 30 90

Website www.izakaya-restaurant.com

IZAKAYA, a culinary hotspot in Amsterdam and authority in Asian gastronomy, takes the traditional Japanese dining experience to a higher level with its famous signature cuisine and subtle South American influences, offered alongside high-quality cocktails in a chic, contemporary setting.

Instock

Czaar Peterstraat 21
1018 Amsterdam
Telephone: +31(0) 20 363 57 65
Website: www.instock.nl

Instock turns surplus food into delicious meals.

De Jonge Dikkert

Amsterdamseweg 104a
1182 HG Amstelveen
Telephone: +31(0) 20 643 33 33
Website: www.jongedikkert.nl

Contemporary international restaurant set within a 17th-century windmill.

JuiceBrothers

Raamsteeg 2
1012 VZ Amsterdam
Van Woustraat 151
1074 AJ Amsterdam
Admiraal de Ruijterweg 4
1056 EX Amsterdam
Binnenhof 6B
1181 ZG Amstelveen
Weesperstraat 101
1018 VN Amsterdam
Gustav Mahlerlaan 24
1082 MC Amsterdam
Telephone: +31(0) 20 362 6492
Website: www.juicebro.com

At JuiceBrothers, our goal is to create quality cold-pressed juice that is nutritious and delicious as hell.

Lavinia Good Food

Kerkstraat 176
1017 GT Amsterdam
Telephone: +31(0) 20 626 14 32
Amstelveenseweg 192
1075 XR Amsterdam
Telephone: +31(0) 20 225 90 29
Main Telephone: +31(0) 20 626 14 50
Website: www.laviniagoodfood.nl

Vegetarian and vegan lunchrooms, serving pure, nutritious food, as well as offering outside catering.

Le Pain Quotidien (Spuistraat)

Spuistraat 266
1012 VW Amsterdam
Telephone: +31(0) 20 622 25 55

Le Pain Quotidien (Nieuwezijds)

Spuistraat 4 H
1012 TS Amsterdam
Telephone: +31(0) 20 891 59 55

Le Pain Quotidien (De Pijp)

Cornelis Troostplein 2 & 4
1072 JK Amsterdam
Telephone: +31(0) 20 675 05 06

Restaurant Lt. Cornelis

Voetboogstraat 13
1012 XK Amsterdam
Telephone: +31(0) 20 261 48 63
Website: www.restaurantcornelis.amsterdam

At Lt. Cornelis you can enjoy a special Dutch meal in a unique atmospheric environment.

Mamouche

Quellijnstraat 104
Amsterdam
1072 XZ
Telephone: +31(0) 20 670 0736
Website: www.restaurantmamouche.nl

A modern take on romantic French dining combined with Moroccan cuisine, capturing the heart of a mother's home-cooking.

MOMO Restaurant, Bar & Lounge

Hobbemastraat 1
1071 XZ Amsterdam
Telephone: +31(0) 20 671 74 74
Website www.momo-amsterdam.com

MOMO is a firm favourite of the Amsterdam culinary scene offering exquisite pan Asian dishes of the highest quality, served in a light-filled contemporary open restaurant with a sleek central bar area and cocktail lounge.

MR PORTER

Spuistraat 175
1012 VN Amsterdam
Telephone: +31(0) 20 811 33 99
Website www.mrportersteakhouse.com

MR PORTER is a fine-dining steakhouse of the highest quality with shared dining at its heart. Its rooftop location offers beautiful views across the city and its high-design restaurant, terrace, lounge and cocktail bar make it one of Amsterdam's most popular restaurants.

Oresti's taverna

Daniel Stalpertstraat 93
1072 XD Amsterdam
Telephone: +31(0) 20 422 27 42
Website: www.orestistaverna.nl

Oresti's taverna is a Mediterranean bar and restaurant in the middle of De Pijp, Amsterdam's Latin Quarter and hot spot for socialising.

The Pancake Bakery

Prinsengracht 191
1015 DS Amsterdam
Telephone: +31(0) 20 625 13 33
Website: www.pancake.nl

The best pancakes in town!

Pasta e Basta
Nieuwe Spiegelstraat 8
1017 DE Amsterdam
Telephone: +31(0) 20 422 22 22
Website: www.pastaebasta.nl
An evening with fantastic dishes, delicious wines and incredible performances by passionate wait staff who provide you with excellent service and sing everything from opera to classics and current songs. Eatertainment!

Pont 13
(Westelijke Houthavens)
Haparandadam 50
1013 AK Amsterdam
Telephone: +31(0) 20 770 27 22
Website: www.pont13.nl
Restaurant on an authentic 1927 ferry in a unique waterfront location.

REM Eiland Restaurant
(Westelijke Houthavens)
Haparandadam 45-2
1013 AK Amsterdam
Telephone: +31(0) 20 688 55 01
Website: www.remeiland.com
A robust restaurant where you can enjoy the taste of great food in the first commercial broadcast station of the Netherlands: REM Eiland.

The Stillery
Telephone: +31(0) 61 660 20 00
Website: www.the-stillery.nl
Amsterdam's most spirited enterprise and creators of The Stillery's First, Dinklewheat Vokda.

Thai Food Cafe
Oranje-Vrijstaatkade 66
Amsterdam
1093 KS
Telephone: +31(0) 20 233 53 64
Website: www.thaifoodcafe.nl
SOI 74
Van Woustraat 74
Amsterdam
1073 LP
Telephone: +31(0) 20 471 0642
Website: www.facebook.com/soi74
They're not fast food, they're street food, authentic, reasonably priced and full of flavour.

VIDA Cervecería Tapería
Valeriusstraat 128b
1075 GD Amsterdam
Telephone: 020 6764647
Website: www.vida.nl
Enjoy the Spanish warmth in the South of Amsterdam.

De Veranda
Amstelveenseweg 764
1081 JK Amsterdam
Telephone: +31(0) 20 644 58 14
Website: www.deveranda.nl
Modern international restaurant on the edge of Amsterdam Forest.

Wild Moa Pies
Topaasstraat 53
1074SZ Amsterdam
Telephone: +31(0) 20 612 61 02
Authentic New Zealand-Australia Shop established since 2001. Inquire for pop-up shop locations or email wildmoapies@gmail.com

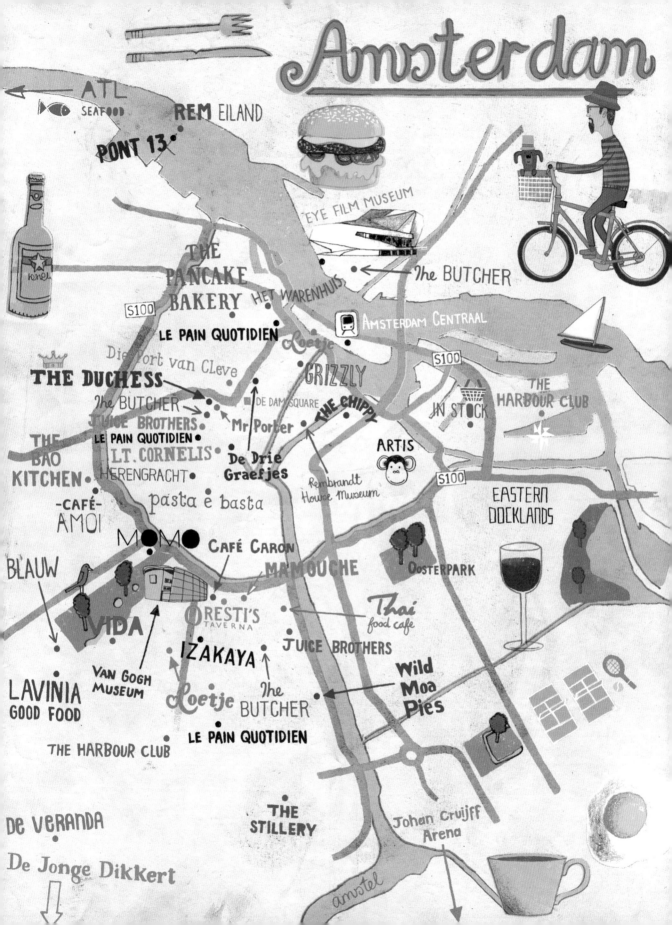

The INDEX

A

Almond
87 Acai almond bowl
127 The Mokum mule

Apple
99 Salted herring with beetroot and apple
111 Bacon and apple pancakes and Lemon and sugar pancakes

Artichoke
83 Old Amsterdam cheese ravioli with cauliflower and hazelnuts

Asam kandis
19 Asam pade with corvina

Asparagus
115 Pork belly bao buns

B

Bacon
27 Biefstuk ossenhaas 'de Roode Waard'
79 Chef Lucas' Wentelteefjes and Bubble and squeak
111 Bacon and apple pancakes

Baking powder
31 Escargots with monkfish fritters

Banana
23 Ikan Pepesan
39 Pain Perdu
79 Chef Lucas' Wentelteefjes
87 Acai almond bowl

Banana leaf
23 Ikan Pepesan

Bay leaves
15 Pork belly bao buns
139 Pulpo horneado

Beef
31 Escargots with monkfish fritters

Beef gravy
31 Escargots with monkfish fritters

Beer
31 Escargots with monkfish fritters
35 Fish and chips

Beetroot
67 Sea bass with groats, beetroot, sea aster, crunchy smelt and sorrel foam
99 Salted herring with beetroot and apple
135 Stuffed free-range chicken from the BBQ with za'atar and hasselback potato

Blue cheese
59 Mac 'n' cheese

Bok choy
131 Vegan pad thai

Brandy
99 Salted herring with beetroot and apple

Bread
39 Pain Perdu
107 Spanakopita

Breadcrumbs
115 Pork belly bao buns

Brown sugar
131 Vegan pad thai

Buttermilk
11 Roasted scallops with fermented garlic mayonnaise and an oriental salad

C

Cabbage
135 Stuffed free-range chicken from the BBQ with za'atar and hasselback potato

Cake
48 Caviar pasta
71 Caramel and sea salt chocolate cake
119 Cheesecake of white chocolate and yoghurt

Capers
35 Fish and chips

Carrot
47 Baby back ribs
67 Sea bass with groats, beetroot, sea aster, crunchy smelt and sorrel foam
95 Chilli sin carne
139 Pulpo horneado

Caster sugar
15 Pork belly bao buns
103 Moroccan chicken pastilla

Cauliflower
83 Old Amsterdam cheese ravioli with cauliflower and hazelnuts

Caviar
48 Caviar pasta
52 Sashimi assortment

Celery
47 Baby back ribs
67 Sea bass with groats, beetroot, sea aster, crunchy smelt and sorrel foam
95 Chilli sin carne and NY Cheesecake
139 Pulpo horneado

Cheese
59 Mac 'n' cheese
67 Sea bass with groats, beetroot, sea aster, crunchy smelt and sorrel foam
95 Chilli sin carne
119 Cheesecake of white chocolate and yoghurt
123 Soufflé of old Amsterdam

Cherry tomato
115 Pork belly bao buns

Chervil
83 Old Amsterdam cheese ravioli with cauliflower and hazelnuts

Chicken

27 Biefstuk ossenhaas 'de Roode Waard'
31 Escargots with monkfish fritters
59 Mac 'n' cheese
83 Old Amsterdam cheese ravioli with cauliflower and hazelnuts
103 Moroccan chicken pastilla
131 Vegan pad thai
135 Stuffed free-range chicken from the BBQ with za'atar and hasselback potato

Chicken liver

135 Stuffed free-range chicken from the BBQ with za'atar and hasselback potato

Chicken stock

31 Escargots with monkfish fritters
83 Old Amsterdam cheese ravioli with cauliflower and hazelnuts
131 Vegan pad thai

Chilli

11 Roasted scallops with fermented garlic mayonnaise and an oriental salad
23 Ikan Pepesan
50 Red chilli and shiso salsa with Dover sole
59 Mac 'n' cheese
115 Green spaghetti with zucchini, asparagus, fresh seafood and panko gremolata
131 Vegan pad thai
143 Awesome lentil and aubergine pie

Chives

139 Pulpo horneado

Chocolate

71 Caramel and sea salt chocolate cake
119 Cheesecake of white chocolate and yoghurt

Cinnamon

39 Pain Perdu
47 Baby back ribs
79 Chef Lucas' Wentelteefjes and Bubble and squeak
103 Moroccan chicken pastilla

Clarified butter

31 Escargots with monkfish fritters

Cocktail

50 Red chilli and shiso salsa with Dover sole
54 Roasted whole leek
127 The Mokum mule

Cod

52 Sashimi assortment

Coriander

11 Roasted scallops with fermented garlic mayonnaise and an oriental salad
63 Ceviche of sea bass
103 Moroccan chicken pastilla
131 Vegan pad thai

Coriander leaves

63 Ceviche of sea bass

Corvina

19 Asam pade with corvina

Cream

11 Roasted scallops with fermented garlic mayonnaise and an oriental salad
31 Escargots with monkfish fritters
35 Fish and chips
48 Caviar pasta
59 Mac 'n' cheese
63 Ceviche of sea bass
67 Sea bass with groats, beetroot, sea aster, crunchy smelt and sorrel foam
71 Caramel and sea salt chocolate cake
79 Chef Lucas' Wentelteefjes and Bubble and squeak
83 Old Amsterdam cheese ravioli with cauliflower and hazelnuts
95 Chilli sin carne and NY Cheesecake
107 Spanakopita
119 Cheesecake of white chocolate and yoghurt

Cream cheese

95 Chilli sin carne and NY Cheesecake
119 Cheesecake of white chocolate and yoghurt

Crème fraiche

67 Sea bass with groats, beetroot, sea aster, crunchy smelt and sorrel foam
83 Old Amsterdam cheese ravioli with cauliflower and hazelnuts

Croissant

79 Chef Lucas' Wentelteefjes and Bubble and squeak

Cucumber

11 Roasted scallops with fermented garlic mayonnaise and an oriental salad
15 Pork belly bao buns
23 Ikan Pepesan

Cumin

95 Chilli sin carne
143 Awesome lentil and aubergine pie

D

Daikon

52 Sashimi assortment

Dark chocolate

71 Caramel and sea salt chocolate cake

Dates

39 Pain Perdu

Dijon mustard

31 Escargots with monkfish fritters

Dill

107 Spanakopita

Double cream

35 Fish and chips

Dover sole

50 Red chilli and shiso salsa with Dover sole

Dried dill

107 Spanakopita

Dried mushroom

83 Old Amsterdam cheese ravioli with cauliflower and hazelnuts

Dried yeast

15 Pork belly bao buns
35 Fish and chips

E

Egg

11 Roasted scallops with fermented garlic mayonnaise and an oriental salad
31 Escargots with monkfish fritters
35 Fish and chips
39 Pain Perdu
75 Famous numbered steak
79 Chef Lucas' Wentelteefjes and bubble and squeak
83 Old Amsterdam cheese ravioli with cauliflower and hazelnuts
95 NY Cheesecake
99 Salted herring with beetroot and apple
107 Spanakopita
123 Soufflé of old Amsterdam
131 Vegan pad thai
135 Stuffed free-range chicken from the BBQ with za'atar and hasselback potato

F

Filo pastry
103 Moroccan chicken pastilla

Firm tofu
95 Chilli sin carne and NY Cheesecake

Fish
11 Roasted scallops with fermented garlic mayonnaise and an oriental salad
19 Asam pade with corvina
23 Ikan Pepesan
35 Fish and chips
52 Sashimi assortment
54 Roasted whole leek
67 Sea bass with groats, beetroot, sea aster, crunchy smelt and sorrel foam
79 Bubble and squeak
99 Salted herring with beetroot and apple

Fish stock
67 Sea bass with groats, beetroot, sea aster, crunchy smelt and sorrel foam

Frozen acai
87 Acai almond bowl

Fructose
95 NY Cheesecake

Fruit
39 Pain Perdu

G

Galangal
19 Asam pade with corvina

Garlic
11 Roasted scallops with fermented garlic mayonnaise and an oriental salad
19 Asam pade with corvina
23 Ikan Pepesan
31 Escargots with monkfish fritters
47 Baby back ribs
54 Roasted whole leek
59 Mac 'n' cheese
67 Sea bass with groats, beetroot, sea aster, crunchy smelt and sorrel foam
95 Chilli sin carne and NY Cheesecake
115 Green spaghetti with zucchini, asparagus, fresh seafood and panko gremolata
131 Vegan pad thai
135 Stuffed free-range chicken from the BBQ with za'atar and hasselback potato
139 Pulpo horneado
143 Awesome lentil and aubergine pie

Garlic powder
47 Baby back ribs
59 Mac 'n' cheese

Gastrique
75 Famous numbered steak

Gelatine
83 Old Amsterdam cheese ravioli with cauliflower and hazelnuts
119 Cheesecake of white chocolate and yoghurt

Ginger
11 Roasted scallops with fermented garlic mayonnaise and an oriental salad
19 Asam pade with corvina
23 Ikan Pepesan
99 Salted herring with beetroot and apple
103 Moroccan chicken pastilla
127 The Mokum mule

Ginger syrup
99 Salted herring with beetroot and apple

Goji berries
87 Acai almond bowl

Granola
87 Acai almond bowl

Grapeseed oil
50 Red chilli and shiso salsa with Dover sole

Green tabasco
50 Red chilli and shiso salsa with Dover sole

Ground ginger
103 Moroccan chicken pastilla

H

Haddock
35 Fish and chips

Hazelnuts
83 Old Amsterdam cheese ravioli with cauliflower and hazelnuts

Herbs
19 Asam pade with corvina
83 Old Amsterdam cheese ravioli with cauliflower and hazelnuts
95 Chilli sin carne

Herring
99 Salted herring with beetroot and apple

Hoisin
15 Pork belly bao buns

Honey
39 Pain Perdu
47 Baby back ribs
87 Acai almond bowl

I

Icing sugar
39 Pain Perdu
79 Chef Lucas' Wentelteefjes
103 Moroccan chicken pastilla
111 Bacon and apple pancakes and Lemon and sugar pancakes

J

Jerusalem artichoke
83 Old Amsterdam cheese ravioli with cauliflower and hazelnuts

K

Kombu
63 Ceviche of sea bass

L

Leek
47 Baby back ribs
54 Roasted whole leek
67 Sea bass with groats, beetroot, sea aster, crunchy smelt and sorrel foam
139 Pulpo horneado

Lemon
11 Roasted scallops with fermented garlic mayonnaise and an oriental salad
19 Asam pade with corvina
23 Ikan Pepesan
31 Escargots with monkfish fritters
35 Fish and chips
48 Caviar pasta
52 Sashimi assortment
54 Roasted whole leek
75 Famous numbered steak
99 Salted herring with beetroot and apple
111 Lemon and sugar pancakes
115 Green spaghetti with zucchini, asparagus, fresh seafood and panko gremolata
139 Pulpo horneado
143 Awesome lentil and aubergine pie

Lemon brandy
99 Salted herring with beetroot and apple

Lemon juice
35 Fish and chips
48 Caviar pasta
54 Roasted whole leek
75 Famous numbered steak
99 Salted herring with beetroot and apple
115 Pork belly bao buns

Lentils
143 Awesome lentil and aubergine pie

Lettuce
59 Mac 'n' cheese

Lime
23 Ikan Pepesan
47 Baby back ribs
50 Red chilli and shiso salsa with Dover sole
52 Sashimi assortment
63 Ceviche of sea bass
115 Green spaghetti with zucchini, asparagus, fresh seafood and panko gremolata
131 Vegan pad thai

M

Mackerel
52 Sashimi assortment

Maldon sea salt
54 Roasted whole leek
71 Caramel and sea salt chocolate cake

Mango
63 Ceviche of sea bass

Margarine
27 Biefstuk ossenhaas 'de Roode Waard'

Mayonnaise
11 Roasted scallops with fermented garlic mayonnaise and an oriental salad
35 Fish and chips
99 Salted herring with beetroot and apple

Milk
15 Pork belly bao buns
39 Pain Perdu
52 Sashimi assortment
59 Mac 'n' cheese
87 Acai almond bowl
111 Bacon and apple pancakes and lemon and sugar pancakes
123 Soufflé of old Amsterdam

Miso
52 Sashimi assortment
95 Chilli sin carne and NY Cheesecake

Monkfish
31 Escargots with monkfish fritters

Mushroom
83 Old Amsterdam cheese ravioli with cauliflower and hazelnuts

Mustard
11 Roasted scallops with fermented garlic mayonnaise and an oriental salad
15 Pork belly bao buns
31 Escargots with monkfish fritters
59 Mac 'n' cheese
99 Salted herring with beetroot and apple

Mustard seeds
15 Pork belly bao buns
99 Salted herring with beetroot and apple

O

Octopus
52 Sashimi assortment
139 Pulpo horneado

Olive oil
11 Roasted scallops with fermented garlic mayonnaise and an oriental salad
31 Escargots with monkfish fritters
35 Fish and chips
50 Red chilli and shiso salsa with Dover sole
54 Roasted whole leek
63 Ceviche of sea bass
67 Sea bass with groats, beetroot, sea aster, crunchy smelt and sorrel foam
79 Bubble and squeak
83 Old Amsterdam cheese ravioli with cauliflower and hazelnuts
95 Chilli sin carne
103 Moroccan chicken pastilla
107 Spanakopita
115 Green spaghetti with zucchini, asparagus, fresh seafood and panko gremolata
139 Pulpo horneado
143 Awesome lentil and aubergine pie

Onion
23 Ikan Pepesan
27 Biefstuk ossenhaas 'de Roode Waard'
47 Baby back ribs
50 Red chilli and shiso salsa with Dover sole
59 Mac 'n' cheese
63 Ceviche of sea bass
99 Salted herring with beetroot and apple
107 Spanakopita
131 Vegan pad thai
139 Pulpo horneado

Onion powder
47 Baby back ribs
59 Mac 'n' cheese

Oyster leaf
52 Sashimi assortment

P

Pad thai
131 Vegan pad thai

Paprika
47 Baby back ribs
59 Mac 'n' cheese
95 Chilli sin carne and NY Cheesecake

Parmesan
59 Mac 'n' cheese
123 Soufflé of old Amsterdam

Parsley
31 Escargots with monkfish fritters
35 Fish and chips
83 Old Amsterdam cheese ravioli with cauliflower and hazelnuts
103 Moroccan chicken pastilla
143 Awesome lentil and aubergine pie

Pasta
48 Caviar pasta
83 Old Amsterdam cheese ravioli with cauliflower and hazelnuts
115 Pork belly bao buns

Peas
35 Fish and chips

Pork
15 Pork belly bao buns
47 Baby back ribs

Pork belly
15 Pork belly bao buns

Porter
54 Roasted whole leek

Potato
11 Roasted scallops with fermented garlic mayonnaise and an oriental salad
35 Fish and chips
135 Stuffed free-range chicken from the BBQ with za'atar and hasselback potato

Purple cauliflower
83 Old Amsterdam cheese ravioli with cauliflower and hazelnuts

R

Raspberries
95 Chilli sin carne and NY Cheesecake

Razor clam
11 Roasted scallops with fermented garlic mayonnaise and an oriental salad

Red onion
50 Red chilli and shiso salsa with Dover sole
63 Ceviche of sea bass

Red pepper
11 Roasted scallops with fermented garlic mayonnaise and an oriental salad
63 Ceviche of sea bass
139 Pulpo horneado

Red shiso vinegar
50 Red chilli and shiso salsa with Dover sole

Rice
19 Asam pade with corvina
23 Ikan Pepesan
52 Sashimi assortment
131 Vegan pad thai

Rice noodles
131 Vegan pad thai

Rice vinegar
52 Sashimi assortment

Rose
107 Spanakopita

Rosemary
115 Pork belly bao buns

S

Saffron
103 Moroccan chicken pastilla

Salad
11 Roasted scallops with fermented garlic mayonnaise and an oriental salad
131 Vegan pad thai

Salmon
52 Sashimi assortment

Sambal ketchup
47 Baby back ribs

Samphire
11 Roasted scallops with fermented garlic mayonnaise and an oriental salad

Sea aster
67 Sea bass with groats, beetroot, sea aster, crunchy smelt and sorrel foam

Sea bass
23 Ikan Pepesan
52 Sashimi assortment
63 Ceviche of sea bass
67 Sea bass with groats, beetroot, sea aster, crunchy smelt and sorrel foam

Seasoning
31 Escargots with monkfish fritters

Shallots
48 Caviar pasta

Shiso leaf
52 Sashimi assortment

Smelt
67 Sea bass with groats, beetroot, sea aster, crunchy smelt and sorrel foam

Smen
103 Moroccan chicken pastilla

Smoked bacon
79 Bubble and squeak

Smoked paprika
47 Baby back ribs
95 Chilli sin carne and NY Cheesecake

Sorrel
67 Sea bass with groats, beetroot, sea aster, crunchy smelt and sorrel foam

Soybean oil
83 Old Amsterdam cheese ravioli with cauliflower and hazelnuts

Soy sauce
63 Ceviche of sea bass
131 Vegan pad thai

Spaghetti
48 Caviar pasta
115 Pork belly bao buns

Sparkling water
35 Fish and chips
67 Sea bass with groats, beetroot, sea aster, crunchy smelt and sorrel foam

Speculoos cookie
95 NY Cheesecake

Spinach
107 Spanakopita

Spring onion
131 Vegan pad thai

Sriracha sauce
15 Pork belly bao buns

Star anise
47 Baby back ribs

Steak
27 Biefstuk ossenhaas 'de Roode Waard'
54 Roasted whole leek
75 Famous numbered steak

Stew
67 Sea bass with groats, beetroot, sea aster, crunchy smelt and sorrel foam

Sushi vinegar
11 Roasted scallops with fermented garlic mayonnaise and an oriental salad

Sweetcorn
95 Chilli sin carne

Tamarind paste
19 Asam pade with corvina
131 Vegan pad thai

T

Tarragon
75 Famous numbered steak
119 Cheesecake of white chocolate and yoghurt
135 Stuffed free-range chicken from the BBQ with za'atar and hasselback potato

Tempura flour
67 Sea bass with groats, beetroot, sea aster, crunchy smelt and sorrel foam

Thyme
48 Caviar pasta
95 Chilli sin carne
115 Green spaghetti with zucchini, asparagus, fresh seafood and panko gremolata
135 Stuffed free-range chicken from the BBQ with za'atar and hasselback potato
143 Awesome lentil and aubergine pie

Tomato
115 Green spaghetti with zucchini, asparagus, fresh seafood and panko gremolata
139 Pulpo horneado

Truffle
11 Roasted scallops with fermented garlic mayonnaise and an oriental salad
123 Soufflé of old Amsterdam

Truffle tapenade
123 Soufflé of old Amsterdam

Turmeric
19 Asam pade with corvina

Turmeric leaf
19 Asam pade with corvina

V

Vanilla
39 Pain Perdu
95 NY Cheesecake

Vanilla extract
95 NY Cheesecake

Vegan
131 Vegan pad thai
143 Awesome lentil and aubergine pie

Vegetable stock
67 Sea bass with groats, beetroot, sea aster, crunchy smelt and sorrel foam
131 Vegan pad thai
143 Awesome lentil and aubergine pie

Vinegar
11 Roasted scallops with fermented garlic mayonnaise and an oriental salad
23 Ikan Pepesan
35 Fish and chips
50 Red chilli and shiso salsa with Dover sole
52 Sashimi assortment
67 Sea bass with groats, beetroot, sea aster, crunchy smelt and sorrel foam
75 Famous numbered steak
83 Old Amsterdam cheese ravioli with cauliflower and hazelnuts
99 Salted herring with beetroot and apple

Vodka
127 The Mokum mule

W

Walnut
127 The Mokum mule

Watercress
31 Escargots with monkfish fritters

Whipped cream
31 Escargots with monkfish fritters

Whipping cream
48 Caviar pasta

White chocolate
119 Cheesecake of white chocolate and yoghurt

White wine
35 Fish and chips
48 Caviar pasta
67 Sea bass with groats, beetroot, sea aster, crunchy smelt and sorrel foam
83 Old Amsterdam cheese ravioli with cauliflower and hazelnuts
99 Salted herring with beetroot and apple
107 Spanakopita
115 Green spaghetti with zucchini, asparagus, fresh seafood and panko

gremolata
131 Vegan pad thai
139 Pulpo horneado

White wine vinegar
35 Fish and chips
67 Sea bass with groats, beetroot, sea aster, crunchy smelt and sorrel foam
83 Old Amsterdam cheese ravioli with cauliflower and hazelnuts

Worcestershire sauce
75 Famous numbered steak

X

Xanthan gum
31 Escargots with monkfish fritters

Y

Yeast
15 Pork belly bao buns
35 Fish and chips

Yellow beetroot
99 Salted herring with beetroot and apple

Yellow tail
52 Sashimi assortment

Yoghurt
119 Cheesecake of white chocolate and yoghurt

Yuzu juice
63 Ceviche of sea bass

Z

Za'atar
135 Stuffed free-range chicken from the BBQ with za'atar and hasselback potato

Other titles in the 'Get Stuck In' series

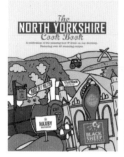

The North Yorkshire Cook Book
features Andrew Pern, Visit York, Made in Malton, Black Sheep Brewery and lots more.
978-1-910863-12-1

The Birmingham Cook Book
features Glynn Purnell, The Smoke Haus, Loaf Bakery, Simpsons and lots more.
978-1-910863-10-7

The Bristol Cook Book
features Dean Edwards, Lido, Clifton Sausage, The Ox, and wines from Corks of Cotham plus lots more.
978-1-910863-14-5

The Oxfordshire Cook Book
features Mike North of The Nut Tree Inn, Sudbury House, Jacobs Inn, The Muddy Duck and lots more.
978-1-910863-08-4

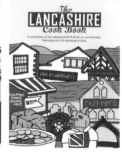

The Lancashire Cook Book
features Andrew Nutter of Nutters Restaurant, Bertram's, The Blue Mallard and lots more.
978-1-910863-09-1

The Liverpool Cook Book
features Burnt Truffle, The Art School, Fraîche, Villaggio Cucina and many more.
978-1-910863-15-2

The Sheffield Cook Book - Second Helpings
features Jameson's Tea Rooms, Craft & Dough, The Wortley Arms, The Holt, Grind Café and lots more.
978-1-910863-16-9

The Leeds Cook Book
features The Boxtree, Crafthouse, Stockdales of Yorkshire and lots more.
978-1-910863-18-3

The Cotswolds Cook Book
features David Everitt-Matthias of Champignon Sauvage, Prithvi, Chef's Dozen and lots more.
978-0-9928981-9-9

The Shropshire Cook Book
features Chris Burt of The Peach Tree, Old Downton Lodge, Shrewsbury Market, CSons and lots more.
978-1-910863-32-9

The Norfolk Cook Book
features Richard Bainbridge, Morston Hall, The Duck Inn and lots more.
978-1-910863-01-5

The Lincolnshire Cook Book
features Colin McGurran of Winteringham Fields, TV chef Rachel Green, San Pietro and lots more.
978-1-910863-05-3

The Newcastle Cook Book
features David Coulson of Peace & Loaf, Bealim House, Grainger Market, Quilliam Brothers and lots more.
978-1-910863-04-6

The Cheshire Cook Book
features Simon Radley of The Chester Grosvenor, The Chef's Table, Great North Pie Co., Harthill Cookery School and lots more.
978-1-910863-07-7

The Leicestershire & Rutland Cook Book
features Tim Hart of Hambleton Hall, John's House, Farndon Fields, Leicester Market, Walter Smith and lots more.
978-0-9928981-8-2

All books in this series are available from Waterstones, Amazon and independent bookshops.

FIND OUT MORE ABOUT US AT WWW.MEZEPUBLISHING.CO.UK